Galton Blackiston

A collection of my favourite recipes
celebrating ten years on the
North Norfolk coast

Published for Morston Hall Hotels Ltd
Morston, Holt, Norfolk, NR25 7AA
Tel: 01263 741041 Fax: 01263 740419
email: reception@morstonhall.com
www. morstonhall.com

By Navigator Guides Ltd
The Old Post Office, Swanton Novers
Melton Constable, Norfolk NR24 2AJ
Tel: 01263 861141 Fax: 01263 861181
email: postmaster@navigatorguides.com
www.navigatorguides.com

Reprinted 2004

Text design Fielding Design
Jacket design Fielding Design

ISBN 1-903872-04-9

A catalogue record for this book is available from the British Library

Colour reproduction by PDQ Digital Media Solutions Ltd, Bungay, Suffolk
Printed in Spain by Mateu Cromo

Galton Blackiston

Recipes from Morston Hall

Photography by Simon Lunt

Acknowledgements

It was my late mother, Anne, who first got me into cooking and for this and many other reasons I would like to dedicate this book to her memory.

My thanks also go to...

My wife Tracy, the brains behind Morston Hall. I may be able to cook, but she has the business acumen, and is the push behind the shove. Tracy has been the continued inspiration to see that we never stand still. For all of this and much more, big thanks.

My father, Bill, for all your support always, and for just being dad.

Tracy's parents, Jan and Rogger Rowe who look after Harry and Sam whenever the going gets tough. We value all your help and support always. And what would we do without the love and support from everyone else in our families too?

All the staff at Morston Hall, especially head chef Sammy, Liz in the office, Isaac out front, and Claire in housekeeping.

Delia and Michael who encouraged us to return to Norfolk and of course for their total commitment to Norwich City Football Club.

Catey Hillier for sharing her editing and writing experiences, and Neil Alston, my right hand man for writing recipes. Without them both this book might not have happened.

Simon Lunt for his inspired photography.

Rupert Wheeler our publisher.

Val, the typist, for patience and perseverance.

All the recipes have been tested by friends in kitchens throughout Norfolk. Your feedback and comments have been vital. Special thanks to Jenny Youngs, and all the following: Neil Alston; Christopher and Lynn Ball; Richard Berrill; Bill Blackiston; David Brookes; William and Jane Carter; Fiona Cattermole; Anne Huggins; Carol Knowles; Lois Murphy; Sheila Parkes; Rosemarie Powell; Pat Read; Mary Roe; Martin Scott; Rebecca Walton; Isobel Wright; Barbara York.

All these folk are excellent cooks: if any of them invite you for supper, accept immediately.

To the following suppliers for providing equipment and props for photography:
ICTC, Norwich
Head Cook & Bottle Washer, North Walsham
Bakers and Larners of Holt
The Linen Barn, Tibenham
Housebait at Burnham Market
Villeroy & Boch

Contents

Starters 63

Fish 85

Foreword

Galton (Spike as I know him), Tracy his wife and I go back a long way. I first met them when they were both working at John Tovey's famous Miller Howe country house hotel in the English Lakes. Galton, as young chef at the beginning of his career, and Tracy front of house. There was an instant rapport, as not only did we share a love of good food and wine, but also a strong mutual passion for Norwich City Football Club, and over the years this has grown into a long-standing friendship.

I was thrilled therefore, years later, when they brought John Tovey's unique tradition of country house hospitality to Morston Hall in Norfolk, adding their own special blend of ideas and creativity.

Since then they have won many awards and accolades, including a much coveted Michelin star, but at the same time, they have remained faithful to the tradition of good home cooking using the finest ingredients.

Here are a collection of Galton's recipes, which he serves at the hotel and demonstrates in his cookery classes, some of them rightly reflecting his John Tovey roots, and others delightfully modern and of the moment. Galton has always been very generous in sharing his ideas and recipes with me and I am therefore honoured and delighted to be able to present and recommend them to you.

Delia Smith
July 2002

From market stall, to Morston Hall

In the summer of 1979, I not only flunked my A levels, but was turned down by my first love: Kent County Cricket Club, where I had high hopes of beinga dashing left-handed batsman. Reality kicked in when my parents told me I had to do something useful. The only thing I was good at – apart from sport – was cooking, and so I started a market stall, Galton's Goodies.

I'd make cakes, jams and breads for Rye market every Thursday, and would invariably sell out by lunchtime. Through the winter it was tough work, so it was music to my ears when my folks got wind of a vacancy in the pastry section of a famous hotel kitchen in the Lake District. At eighteen I got the job at Miller Howe, and started cooking in my first professional kitchen under the tutorage of John Tovey.

It was at Miller Howe that I got the nickname Spike because of my cropped hair, and the fact that JT and others always said that Galton was a nightmare to pronounce.

It was also there that I first met Delia; at a party celebrating the sale of her millionth cookery book we got chatting, as she had heard that a fellow Norwich City supporter was working in the kitchen, and as we all know there aren't too many of us Canaries around!

Another important lady came into my life at Miller Howe: Tracy the restaurant manageress, now my wonderful wife. By this time I was head chef – a title I knew would impress her at the staff party, where we first got together. A year on, in December 1987, we combined our talents in marriage.

Two years later, my parents drove past Morston Hall and noticing the for sale sign, phoned to tell us. We'd always had ambitions on our own place, and Delia and her husband Michael were encouraging us to come south.

Our dreams finally came true in the spring of 1992 with the help of our then business partner Justin Fraser. We opened with just four bedrooms, having scrimped and borrowed from friends and families. We were very fortunate at that time to have Robin and Ian Fraser as our friendly financiers, both sets of parents supporting us throughout and my oldest brother Andrew sorting out the legalities. Yes, it was an almighty struggle, but the lure of returning to Norfolk – my backyard – was too strong to resist.

We got slaughtered by the *Daily Telegraph* in our first restaurant review – the prompt for a bit of a re-think. The rest, as they say, is history, and we've had ten amazing years since.

Simplicity, the art of good food

Simple things done well are better than complicated things done badly. The rule of the Morston Hall kitchen has always been: keep it simple and keep itfresh. As I have got older, I am more concerned with cooking good basic ingredients simply.

Loads of people ask why we have a set menu at Morston. From what I'd been told about north Norfolk before we opened, I'd imagined the quality of produce was going to be a problem. By sticking to a set menu, I figured that the food would be as fresh as possible every single night of the week. If I knew then what I know now, things may have been different.....

The aim of this book is to help you take your cooking a stage further. Everyone can cook– commonsense and an unswerving ambition to cook to the best of your ability are all that's needed; that's pretty much what I've relied on all these years!

It is important, however, that you have an understanding of these recipes: do read them right through before you begin. Just as importantly, you must have time to cook – these are not quick fix recipes to be done in minutes – some require time and care, but most can be done in stages. Good *mise en place* is important too – remember it is often the preparation that takes the time, not the actual cooking.

So why publish this book? After a decade of running a quietly successful business with my wife Tracy, the little ring of confidence that perhaps wasn't there all those years ago now has a little more sparkle and luminescence.

My goodness, this book has been a long time coming. I remember being asked by an enthusiastic group attending one of my early cookery courses not long after opening Morston Hall, 'well Galton, what about doing a book of your recipes?'

Ten years on – here it is.

Galton Blackiston
July 2002

'*Most kitchens are hot houses where temperatures rise. Concentration, dedication and consistency are what we aim for .*'

Photographs shot at 7.45pm, 11 July 2002
Another busy evening in the Morston kitchen

An A-Z of Useful Information

A good sharp knife is essential for any would be cook. It is worth a dozen blunt ones and you'll certainly cut yourself less often.

Blowtorch For caramelising a creme brulee or browning the top of an apple tart, a blowtorch is a useful piece of kit for anyone's kitchen. Always use it carefully though and keep it well away from children. You can get specialist ones in kitchenware shops, but I prefer using a plumber's blow torch, as it is more powerful. They are available from all good builders' merchants.

Cooking When writing this book I have assumed that readers have a basic knowledge of cooking. It is not a book for novices. However, if you should like to learn more, why not book up on one of the Morston Hall cookery courses.

Cooking Times Remember, cooking times should be treated as a guide only, as all appliances vary. Check your oven is performing consistently by using an oven thermometer. Cooking times have all been tested in these recipes. However, always check by looking, smelling and touching the food to see for yourself whether it is cooked correctly.

Eggs Medium-sized eggs were used for testing these recipes.

Equipment Use a **food mixer** for mixing, whisking and combining ingredients. You can buy a pasta-making attachment for your electric food mixer and, after many years without one, I now realise how useful they can be.
A **food processor** does just what it says. It cannot be used in place of a food mixer, as the processing action is too intense.
Use a **blender** to puree and liquidise.
A **hand-held electric whisk** will allow you to work with smaller quantities of ingredients. It also gives you more of a feel for what is going on in the bowl.
Ice cream machines are an expensive luxury where you do get what you pay for. The Gelato machine churns and freezes the mixture, and this is the one I would recommend.

Flour As a general rule I always use strong plain flour for bread making, and soft plain flour for both sweet and savoury pastry.

Herbs All the recipes which use herbs in this book refer to fresh rather than dried. If you use fresh herbs wherever possible you'll always get a better result.

Ice Cream and Sorbets If you don't have an ice cream machine, freeze the mixture in a shallow container. And then as it freezes you must remember to whisk it thoroughly at least four times. The more you whisk the ice cream, the smoother the end result.
Ice creams and sorbets should be taken out of the freezer well before serving. As a guide, 20 minutes is about right to allow it to be more easily scooped and bring out the flavours.

Milk I always use full fat milk for cooking.

Mise en Place This simply means 'to put in place' and is the kitchen term for prepping up ingredients. Many of the recipes in this book require plenty of advance preparation, so get your mise en place ready and you'll have fewer last minute hassles at the stove.

Reading It is important before attempting a recipe that you read it thoroughly from start to finish to ensure you understand it and are familiar with it.

Seasoning To season means adding salt and pepper to taste, unless otherwise stated. Always season sparingly – you can add more salt and pepper, but you cannot remove it.

Tasting As you work through a recipe, do taste as you go along.

Vegetables To cook vegetables briefly, plunge them into boiling salted water. This technique is known as blanching.
To halt the cooking and retain the colour, plunge the blanched vegetables into cold running water. This is known as refreshing.

Weights and Measures The recipes in this book are written using metric and imperial measurements. Approximate conversions have been used and they have either been rounded up or down.
Never mix metric and imperial measurements in one recipe.
Personally I still work in pounds and ounces when I'm cooking.
Spoon measures should always be level.

Breads, Pastry, Biscuits and Pasta

Unfortunately I could recite the recipe for shortcrust pastry at the tender age of 17 – sad, but absolutely true. My mother insisted that I learned the family recipe off by heart in order to secure my first job in a professional kitchen. On the long train journey to Miller Howe, from Kent to Windermere, I repeated the recipe over and over again to her, until I could recite it like a poem.

Now I'm not suggesting that you go so far as to learn the recipes in this chapter word for word, but it does help if you adhere to a few ground rules.

Bread-making tips

Firstly, any liquids you use must not be too hot, as too high a temperature kills the yeast. After all you want the yeast to work well, as this is in fact what makes your bread rise. In the same way you'd test the temperature of a baby's bath water, use your little finger to gauge if the liquid is hand warm and therefore fine for the yeast to work its magic.

Fresh yeast produces better bread, full stop. In fact I don't even know how to use dried yeast. I would recommend that you always use fresh: it is easy to use and you won't pick up any of those musty yeasty flavours in the resulting bread.

Making bread has always been part of our daily routine at Morston Hall, seven days a week. When we first started ten years ago, one white bread roll was the order of the day for each diner. However, such was the appreciative response to our bread-making efforts that we now make a dozen different varieties and everyone can take as much as they dare.

I accept most households would not bake bread every day, but it is really worth making a few loaves for special occasions. All these bread recipes will freeze well, too, so one session in the kitchen will be all you need to create a stash in your freezer. Remember, once you get hooked on bread-making – and it really is a rather satisfying job – the bought in stuff never quite tastes the same again.

Better pastry

To make good pastry, good-quality ingredients – especially good-quality butter – are more important than having cold hands. Let's knock that old wives' tale on the head straight away.

A light touch is important as well. It is essential to work your dough carefully and not to overhandle it. I say always use your hands for pastry making – they will produce better results than any piece of kit. The only exception would be when making puff pastry, where a food mixer – not a processor – does come in handy.

Pastry making *is* easy. Again, take heed of a few simple kitchen rules, and you'll do just fine.

Remember that you must rest pastry dough in the fridge after you've made it; again after it has been worked; and, again, before it is cooked.

I got the tip for chilling pastry in a long sausage shape, rather than a big square block, from some of our young kitchen staff, fresh out of college. This way, they told me, it warms up more quickly and is ready to use. The advice holds true whether you are resting pastry or freezing it.

For the best results, always prick pastry dough before cooking. This allows it to breathe and therefore stops any bubbles. The exception would be filled tarts, such as lemon or egg custard, where the pastry case must be sealed.

And what about creating neat pastry edges on a flan? My advice is: cook it, and then trim it. By baking pastry with the edges hanging over the edge of the flan ring, you allow for shrinkage and create a cleaner, neater edge.

Be a pasta master

If you have the time and the inclination it is worth the challenge of making your own pasta. I suggest you'll need to be in the right mood though: it can be a bit of a laborious process, but the end result will be worth it. Rather than use a hand-rolling machine, you'll really save time if you invest in a pasta-making attachment for your electric mixer. Another tip, Italian double zero flour is best, but if you can't get your hands on a bag, strong plain flour will work just as well.

Brioche

Makes 2 x 900 g (2 lb)

loaves or 20 rolls

6 tbsp milk

50 g (2 oz) caster sugar

40 g (1½ oz) fresh yeast

500 g (18 oz) strong plain flour,

sieved

110 g (4 oz) unsalted butter,

cut into small pieces

1 level tsp salt

4 eggs

1 egg yolk to glaze

If I had to order my very last supper, it would have to include hot toasted brioche with foie gras. And, if the budget wouldn't stretch to foie gras, or if it was unavailable – given the concerns over its production – hot toasted brioche spread generously with butter would do nicely.

Method

Pour the milk into a small saucepan, add 2 teaspoonfuls of the sugar and gently heat until just warmed. Take care not to have the milk too hot. If this does happen, then allow to cool before adding the yeast. Mash the yeast in a medium sized bowl and add the warm milk, mixing thoroughly. Add 50 g (2 oz) of the strong plain flour and whisk together. Cover with a cloth and allow to froth up. This will take about 10 minutes. Place the remaining sugar, flour, salt and unsalted butter in the bowl of a food mixer. Using the k beater attachment, slowly bind together.

Once the yeast mixture is frothy, add 4 eggs and whisk gently. Pour this into the flour mixture and continue to beat until well blended and a light dough has formed. Leave the machine to knead slowly for a good 5 minutes. Cover the bowl with a damp cloth, and leave the dough to prove somewhere warm until it has doubled in size. This will take at least an hour. Turn out onto a floured surface and continue kneading well by hand for 2 minutes.

Line 2 x 900 g (2 lb) loaf tins with greaseproof paper. Alternatively, use non-stick tins. Halve the dough and put into the prepared tins. Place somewhere warm to prove again for about 40 minutes, until the dough rises to the top of the tins.

Pre-heat the oven to 200C/400F/Gas 6. Once the dough has hit the top of the loaf tin, brush with the beaten egg yolk. Place in the oven and bake for about 20 minutes, until the loaves are a deep golden colour. The loaves will develop a very dark crust, which is characteristic of brioche. Don't worry, it is due to the quantity of eggs used. Finally, remove from the oven and turn out onto a cooling rack. Serve lightly toasted with savoury pates and terrines, or with marmalade for breakfast.

Our Very Popular Wholemeal Bread

Makes 2 x 900 g (2 lb)

loaves

700 g (1½ lbs) wholemeal flour

225 g (½ lb) strong plain flour,

sifted

110 g (4 oz) muesli, select a

luxury fruity mix

10 g (½ oz) sea salt

4 tbsp black treacle

725 ml (1¼ pints) warm water

50 g (2 oz) fresh baker's yeast

2 x 900 g (2 lb) loaf tins lined

with greaseproof paper

Rest assured, this recipe will soon become as popular in your kitchen as it has in mine over the past 10 years. And, if you've never made bread before, this is a great place to start: the dough requires only one proving, making it considerably quicker and easier than most breads. It is dense and sweet – ideal for toasting at breakfast. We do in fact get more requests for this recipe than anything from the breakfast table, and every week customers order loaf after loaf to take home. I'll happily make you a loaf, but please place your order with the waiting staff as I'm not at my best in the mornings – especially if we've been celebrating a Norwich victory the night before.

Method

Place the 2 flours, muesli and salt in the bowl of a food mixer with the k beater or dough hook attachment. In a measuring jug melt the treacle thoroughly with the warm water. Crumble the yeast on top of the liquid and leave to froth until it resembles the head of a pint of Guinness. Turn the food mixer on to a low speed and slowly pour the liquid into the flour and muesli mixture so that it binds together. Leave the machine running for a further 5 minutes.

The end result should be a sloppy dough mix, which is just right for loaves of bread, but too wet to adapt to make bread rolls. Divide the dough mixture equally between the 2 lined loaf tins and pat down gently. Place somewhere warm to prove for about 30 minutes, or until the dough has risen to the top of the tins.

Pre-heat the oven to 200C/400F/Gas 6. Bake the loaves for 30–40 minutes. Remove from the oven and turn out onto a cooling rack.

Serve hot, toasted for breakfast, or thinly sliced with smoked salmon.

Shallot, Olive and Rosemary Bread

Makes 2 loaves

40 g (1½ oz) fresh yeast

1 tsp caster sugar

275 ml (½ pint) warm water

1 egg, beaten

150 ml (¼ pint) milk

700 g (1½ lbs) strong plain flour

1 tsp salt

50 g (2 oz) salted butter

*75 g (3 oz) black olives, stoned
and halved*

2 sprigs rosemary

*2 shallots, peeled and thickly
sliced*

*Good olive oil to drizzle over the
dough*

2 tbsp coarse sea salt

You don't need Italian blood to make that ever-popular Italian flatbread, foccacia. But reading the recipes of a much-respected Italian hero of mine, Franco Taruschio, now retired from The Walnut Tree in Abergavenny, provided the inspiration to come up with a North Norfolk version. Thyme is a good substitute if you don't have rosemary. Thankfully at Morston we always have plenty of both. Folk say that if the lady of the house wears the trousers, then the herb garden will always be bountiful. Enough said.

Method

Begin by combining the yeast and sugar in a bowl. Mix with your fingertips so that the yeast breaks down and becomes smooth and almost liquid. Then add 275 ml (½ pint) of warm water. Mix well and add the beaten egg and milk. Set aside.

In a food mixer blend the flour, salt and butter on a slow speed using the dough hook or a k beater. Add the liquid yeast a little at a time, slowly turning the speed up. However, you may find that you do not require all the liquid. The end result you are working towards is dough that has a texture that does not stick to your fingers when they are pushed into it. I usually leave the dough mixing in the machine for 8–10 minutes. Once you are happy with the texture, turn the machine off and remove the paddle. Cover the dough with a clean, damp cloth.

Place the mixing bowl somewhere warm for the dough to prove, until it has doubled in volume. This will usually take at least an hour. Turn the dough out onto a lightly floured surface and knead.

Divide into two equal sized loaves and place on a large greaseproof-covered baking tray, leaving room for the dough to rise again. Pierce the dough at 2.5 cm (1 inch) intervals pushing into it, right to the bottom, an olive, a sprig of fresh rosemary and a large slice of shallot, in that order, making sure that the olive is at the bottom. Finally, liberally drizzle the top of the loaves with olive oil, and sprinkle with flakes of sea salt.

Pre-heat the oven to 220C/425F/Gas 7. Allow the dough to prove again until doubled in size. This should take around 45 minutes in a warm place. Bake for about 20–25 minutes until a deep golden colour. The loaf should sound quite hollow when tapped with your knuckles. Allow to cool. Just before serving, reheat the bread in an oven pre-heated to 200C/400F/Gas 6 for 5 minutes, drizzle the top with yet more olive oil, slice the bread thickly and serve warm.

White Bread Rolls

Makes 16 to 20 rolls

450 g (1 lb) strong plain flour

1 tsp salt

75 g (3 oz) salted butter

100 ml (3½ fl oz) warm water

100 ml (3½ fl oz) warm milk

1 egg, beaten

25 g (1 oz) fresh yeast

1 tbsp caster sugar

50 g (2 oz) poppy or sesame

seeds

If you want to join the bread-making fraternity, here's a no frills recipe that will get you off to a good start. Once you've had success with this, you can quickly progress by adapting this basic recipe to whatever your tastebuds desire – from poppy seed rolls to sauteed onions, grated cheese, or walnuts.

Method

Sift the flour and salt into the bowl of a food mixer and with a k beater or dough hook attachment combine together with the butter. Leave the mixer running on slow for minutes. Mix the warm water and milk together with the beaten egg. The mixture should make 275 ml (½ pint). In a separate bowl cream together the yeast and caster sugar, then add the mixed liquids. Next, slowly pour the liquid into the flour with the machine still running.

The mixture will bind together and within about 5 minutes will eventually form smooth, soft dough. What you are working towards is dough that has a texture that does not stick to your fingers when they are pushed into it. Take the bowl off the machine, cover with a damp tea towel and place somewhere warm to prove until doubled in size, approximately 45 minutes.

Turn the dough out onto a floured surface, knead well and cut into 16–20 portions and shape into rolls. Place on a baking sheet lined with greaseproof paper leaving space between them. You can top the rolls with poppy or sesame seeds at this stage by brushing them with beaten egg and dipping the rolls into the seeds. For other flavours, I also recommend crushed coriander seeds or salt flakes. Without covering, leave to prove in a warm place, until the rolls double in size.

Pre-heat the oven to 220C/425F/Gas 7. When the dough has risen sufficiently place in the hot oven and bake for approximately 15–20 minutes until golden brown.

Choux Pastry

Makes 20–24 eclairs

50 g (2 oz) butter

150 ml (¼ pint) cold water

3 tsp sugar

60 g (2½ oz) strong plain flour,
  sieved

2 eggs, beaten

Maybe because of its French name, there's always an element of mystery about this recipe. There shouldn't be – it is easy to make, so do have a go. If you're in the know, you'll realise choux pastry is right back in fashion too. If you want to be rather risque, deep-fry a tiny ball of choux dough and watch it puff up in front of your eyes into a French doughnut. Dredge in caster sugar and then let it melt in your mouth.

Method

In a saucepan, melt the butter with the water and sugar. Heat gently and, once the butter has melted, add the flour. Beat well with a wooden spoon. Take out of the pan and place in a bowl. Using an electric hand whisk, on high speed, slowly add the eggs. Every so often push down the mixture around the outside of the bowl with a spatula, and continue whisking until you have a smooth, fairly thick batter.

Pre-heat the oven to 200C/400F/Gas 6. Place a piece of greaseproof paper onto a flat baking tray. Using a piping bag with a 1 cm (½ inch) plain round nozzle, pipe lengths about 5 mm (2 inch) long, leaving enough room in between for the eclairs to expand. Just prior to putting the tray in the oven, dab the baking sheet with a little water. Place in the oven for about 10–15 minutes until golden. Then, turn the oven off, and leave the eclairs for about 5 minutes to dry out. Remove from the oven and leave to cool on a wire rack.

To serve, either make a coffee icing using 3 tablespoons 'Camp' coffee and 110 g (4 oz) icing sugar beaten together to coat the top of the eclairs, or, melt some chocolate in a bowl over a saucepan of hot water, add a knob of butter and dip the eclairs in. At Morston Hall, I split the eclairs and fill them with creme patissiere, but fresh whipped cream will do very nicely.

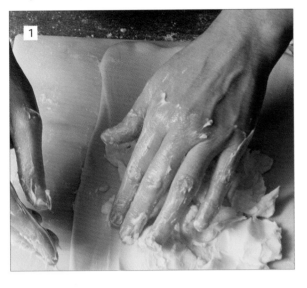

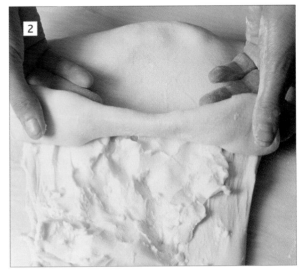

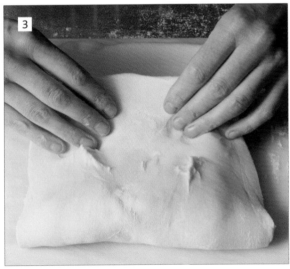

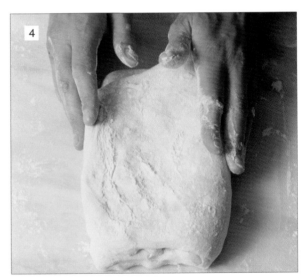

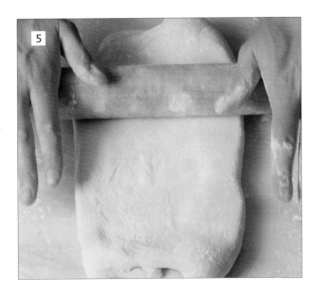

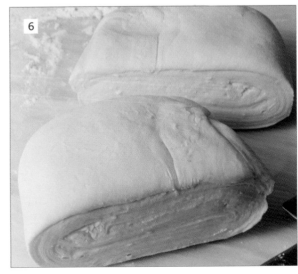

Classic Puff Pastry

Makes 4 x 275 g (10 oz)

blocks of puff pastry

475 g (1 lb 1 oz) strong plain

flour

1 tsp salt

450 g (1 lb) unsalted butter,

slightly softened

ice cold water and

1 tbsp lemon juice

1 tbsp white wine vinegar

combined to make 275 ml

(½ pint)

Method

Sift the flour and salt into the bowl of a food mixer, add 125 g (4 oz) of the butter and combine with the k beater or dough hook. Mix the water, lemon juice and white wine vinegar in a jug to make 275 ml (½ pint) and slowly pour into the flour mixture. Continue to mix slowly with the k beater or dough hook until the dough is pliable – like bread dough – and doesn't stick to the sides of the bowl.

Take the dough out of the bowl, place onto a tray, cover with a dry cloth and refrigerate for about half an hour.

Roll out the pastry away from you into a rectangular shape about 50 cm x 25 cm (20 inch x 10 inch). Spread the remaining butter over two-thirds of the pastry at the top end, patting it down gently, whilst avoiding going too close to the edges (*see* photo 1). Fold up the bottom third of the pastry, which has not been coated with butter, onto the middle section (*see* photo 2). Then fold down the remaining third of buttered pastry over the top of this, to create a sandwich of pastry (*see* photo 3).

Lightly flour the pastry. Turn the pastry block a quarter turn to the right (*see* photo 4), and again roll away from you, firmly and evenly so the pastry becomes about twice its original length (*see* photo 5).

In the same way, fold the pastry into three again, bringing the top third down to the middle and then folding the bottom third on top.

Now give the pastry a quarter turn to the right again and repeat the rolling and folding procedure once more, making sure the pastry doesn't stick to the work surface.

Brush off any excess flour with a pastry brush. Try to keep the edges neat and as straight as possible. Wrap in clingfilm and chill in the fridge for 20 minutes.

Repeat the rolling, folding and chilling process 4 times more, remembering to turn the pastry a quarter turn to the right after each procedure. Don't forget to rest the pastry for at least 20 minutes in the fridge after every 2 rollouts.

Finally rest the pastry in the fridge until ready to use. Cut it into 4 blocks and refrigerate or freeze (*see* photo 6, the finished pastry).

Sweet Pastry

Makes sufficient to line

3 x 20 cm (8 inch) flan tins

310 g (11 oz) plain flour

150 g (5 oz) caster sugar

pinch of salt

175 g (6 oz) unsalted butter,

softened

3 egg yolks

few drops of vanilla essence

3 tbsp water

Use this pastry recipe (photographed opposite) if you are making the Classic Lemon Tart or Egg Custard Tart (*see* recipes, pages 149 and 153).

Method

Sift together the flour, sugar and salt in a large bowl. Add the butter in small knobs and, using your fingertips, combine the mixture to produce fine breadcrumbs. Beat the egg yolks together and add the vanilla. Drizzle this into the flour mixture, followed by the water, and gently bring it all together to produce a soft dough. Turn out onto a lightly floured surface. The pastry mixture will be soft to the touch.

Divide the pastry into three and individually wrap in clingfilm. Refrigerate for at least an hour, or freeze for use at a later stage. Each third will be sufficient to cover a 20 cm (8 inch) fluted or plain flan tin.

Once the dough has been chilled in the fridge (or has been defrosted from the freezer) you can treat it quite vigorously, moulding it in your hands to make it pliable.

To line the tin, first roll the pastry directly onto the flan base (*see* photos 1, 2 and 3).

Fold the excess pastry onto itself (photo 4), and return the base to the flan ring (photo 5). Unfold the pastry (photo 6) and, using a ball of excess pastry, press the lining into the grooves of the flan tin (photo 7). Place beans into the flan tin for baking (photo 8). Finally, seal any cracks in the cooked pastry with egg yolk (photo 9).

Savoury Pastry

Makes sufficient to line

2 x 20 cm (8 inch) flan tins

225 g (8 oz) plain flour, sifted

pinch of salt

1 tsp icing sugar

50 g (2 oz) salted butter

50 g (2 oz) lard

1 egg yolk, beaten with 2 tbsp

cold water

This is an excellent, extremely versatile pastry, which can be used for quiches, savoury tarts and canape bases. It freezes well, too.

Method

Sift the flour, salt and sugar into a large mixing bowl. Add the knobs of softened butter and lard, and with your fingertips rub into the flour until the mixture resembles fine breadcrumbs. Drizzle the egg yolk and water over the surface and gently bind together, to produce a soft dough, which is not too sticky.

Turn onto a floured surface and divide into 2. Wrap each half in clingfilm and refrigerate for at least an hour. At this point you can freeze the pastry to use later.

Scones

Makes 6–8 scones

225 g (8 oz) self-raising flour

½ tsp baking powder

½ tsp bicarbonate of soda

50 g (2 oz) caster sugar

40 g (1½ oz) salted butter,

softened

handful of sultanas

150 ml (¼ pint) milk, but you

may need up to 175 ml

(6 fl oz)

1 egg yolk, beaten with a touch

of milk for an egg wash

My rather flamboyant boss at Miller Howe, the legendary John Tovey, used to say: 'If you've got it, then flaunt it!' If your scones rise like mine, then you'll certainly have got it.

Method

Pre-heat the oven to 200C/400F/Gas 6. In a large bowl sift together the flour, baking powder and bicarbonate of soda, then finally add the sugar. Break the softened butter into the flour and, with your fingertips, rub in so the mixture resembles fine breadcrumbs. Add the sultanas, then slowly add the milk. By gently coaxing the mixture with your hands, bring the dough together. The end result should be a slightly sticky, but reasonably firm, dough.

Place the dough on a lightly floured surface, mould into a flat round shape about 2 cm (¾ inch) thick using a rolling pin or the flat of your hand. Using a plain 6 cm (2½ inch) pastry cutter cut out 6–8 rounds and place the scones on to a baking sheet. Carefully brush only the top of the scones with the eggwash, and place in the oven for 10–15 minutes.

At Morston Hall I always serve scones with lashings of clotted cream and home-made jam – altogether an indulgent afternoon teatime treat.

Parmesan Cheese Biscuits

Makes about 90 biscuits

225 g (8 oz) plain flour

225 g (8 oz) Parmesan, finely
grated (ready bought packet
Parmesan is ideal)

225 g (8 oz) salted butter

salt and pepper

good pinch of cayenne pepper

225 g (8 oz) mature Cheddar,
finely grated

Method

Sieve the soft plain flour into a large mixing bowl, and add the finely grated Parmesan. Break in knobs of butter and with your fingertips gently rub in to achieve a paste that does not stick to your fingers. Season lightly and then add a good pinch of cayenne pepper. Finally mix in the grated Cheddar, and gently work together to form a dough. Divide into 3 balls, wrap each individually in clingfilm and refrigerate for at least an hour before using.

Pre-heat the oven to 180C/350F/Gas 4. Mould the pastry well in your hands before rolling, as this will make it much more pliable.

On a lightly floured surface, roll out to about 3 mm (⅛ inch) thick. Using a round pastry cutter, cut out biscuits approximately 5 cm (2 inches) in diameter. Using a palette knife, transfer the biscuits to a baking tray lined with greaseproof paper. Prick all over and chill in the fridge for 20 minutes. Finally, bake in the oven for about 15 minutes until the biscuits are a light golden colour. Allow to cool before removing from the tray.

Orange and Almond Snaps

Makes about 20 biscuits

110 g (4 oz) flaked almonds

110 g (4 oz) caster sugar

50 g (2 oz) plain flour, sieved

75 g (3 oz) unsalted butter

rind and juice of a small orange,
blood oranges are perfect

Method

Roughly chop the almonds and place in a bowl with the sugar and plain flour. In a separate bowl, melt the butter, and add the juice and rind of the orange. Add the orange butter mixture to the almonds, sugar and flour and beat with a wooden spoon. Refrigerate for 1 hour.

Pre-heat the oven to 180C/350F/Gas 4. Cover a baking tray with a non-stick baking sheet. Spoon 6 nuggets, about the size of a walnut, onto the baking sheet leaving plenty of space between them, as they will spread whilst cooking. Place in the oven and bake for about 12 minutes or until they are golden brown. Remove from the oven and allow to cool.

When cooled, store the biscuits in an airtight container. However, they are best eaten on the day of making.

Sesame and Poppy Seed Crisps

Makes 26 biscuits

75 g (3 oz) unsalted butter

75 g (3 oz) caster sugar

3 tsp liquid glucose

30 ml (1 fl oz) milk

25 g (1 oz) poppy seeds

75 g (3 oz) sesame seeds

Method

Melt the butter, sugar, glucose and milk in a saucepan over a low heat. Stir in the seeds. Take off the heat and pour into a bowl. Leave to cool for at least a couple of hours.

Pre-heat the oven to 180C/350F/Gas 4. Line a baking tray with a non-stick baking sheet. Using a teaspoon make little balls of the mixture and place onto the tray, leaving plenty of space between them. Push down with your thumb to flatten. It is best not to put too many on the tray at once.

Bake in the pre-heated oven for about 10 minutes, until golden brown. Take out of the oven and allow to cool before removing from the tray with a palette knife. While the biscuits are still warm, lay them over a rolling pin so they become curved. Store in an airtight container. The biscuits are, however, best eaten on the day they were made.

Viennese Biscuits

Makes about 26 biscuits

225 g (8 oz) salted butter,
  softened

50 g (2 oz) icing sugar, sifted

225 g (8 oz) plain flour, sifted

vanilla sugar to sprinkle over
  biscuits

We serve a ton of these much-loved Morston favourites with morning coffee every day. It really is one of the easiest recipes to master, but remember – use unsalted butter at your peril: it makes the biscuits far too crumbly – don't ask me why, it just does.

Method

Pre-heat the oven to 180C/350F/Gas 4. Cover 2 medium sized baking trays with non-stick baking paper. Cream the salted butter and icing sugar together until very light in colour and fluffy – an electric hand whisk is ideal for this. Finally, slowly whisk in the sifted flour.

Put the mixture into a piping bag with a star shaped nozzle, and pipe out approximately 26 x 5 cm (2 inch) strips onto the baking trays. Leave plenty of space between them as they do spread while cooking.

Bake in the pre-heated oven for about 15 minutes until the biscuits are a golden colour. Take out and sprinkle with vanilla caster sugar while still warm. Leave the biscuits to cool. Store in an airtight container. However, the biscuits are really at their best when freshly made, and so should be eaten on the same day.

Homemade Pasta

Serves 6

250 g (9 oz) 00 pasta flour or

strong plain flour

9 yolks from medium eggs

1 whole medium egg

pinch of salt

2 tsp olive oil

When you can buy such good-quality fresh pasta, this recipe may seem like a lot of work. But believe me, it is worth the effort as the end result will be better than anything you can buy. A pasta machine, or a mixer attachment, is essential to do this recipe, so put one on your Christmas wish list right now.

Method

Sift the flour and salt into the bowl of a food processor. Lightly beat all the yolks and the whole egg, plus the olive oil, in a jug. Turn on the food processor and quickly pour the eggs and oil into the flour, so that it comes together as a crumbly textured dough.

Turn the machine off, take out the pasta dough and knead it into a ball by hand. The dough should have a smooth appearance. Cover with clingfilm, and leave to rest in the fridge for at least an hour.

The next stage involves a pasta machine. Cut the pasta dough into 5 pieces. Take one of the pieces and, on a lightly floured surface, flatten it with your hands or a rolling pin.

Set the pasta machine to setting 1 (widest setting) and roll through this piece of pasta dough (*see* photo 1). Fold the strip in half, lightly flour it and roll it through the machine again on the same setting. Do this seven times. Then set the machine to setting 2, lightly flour the dough and roll it through to lengthen the piece of dough. Do not fold the dough any further. Next set the machine to number 3 and once again roll through the lightly floured strip of pasta dough. Continue to roll out the dough in the same way, without folding it, right up to setting number 7 (photo 2).

Repeat this rolling out process for each piece of dough and you will finish up with five very long strips of pasta. At this stage a wooden broom handle or a wooden clothes horse to hang the strips on will become your best friend.

Finally, using either the angel hair or tagliatelle rollers on your pasta machine, roll the strips of pasta through for the last time (photo 3). Hang the strips over the clothes horse (photo 4).

This freshly made pasta needs very little cooking; do so in plenty of fiercely boiling salted water, and always drain thoroughly. Finally, stir through a little extra virgin olive oil or butter or, my favourite, some freshly chopped chives.

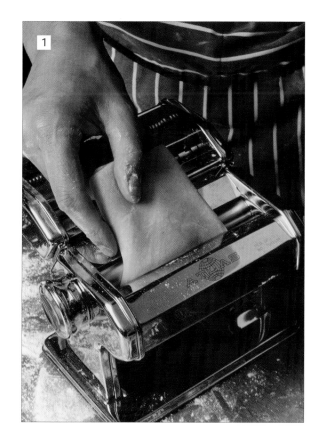

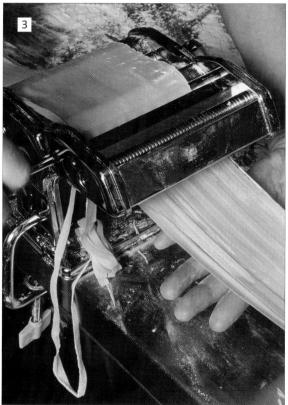

Stocks, Sauces and Soups

Years ago – as all young chefs were taught back then – I tended to thicken my sauces with flour. That's all I knew. And it wasn't until starting our own business – and getting an absolutely scathing restaurant review in *The Daily Telegraph* within the first month of opening Morston Hall – that I realised the way to make stocks and sauces had moved on big time. My whole training had to change overnight.

That bad review provided the impetus to rework the way the kitchen made gravy, and get to grips with more classical techniques for stock-making. So I read lots, talked to other cooks about what they did, and we gradually evolved our style of stocks, sauces and soups.

To think of those dark, floury sauces now really makes me cringe. The lesson, though, is that you never stop learning in the kitchen.

So, in this chapter, I want to remind you how easy it is to make stocks, sauces and soups, and especially to show you how good stock will really enhance the flavour of your cooking.

Good stock equals good flavour

Believe me, leftover bones from chicken, beef or lamb are best converted into stock. Ask your butcher to save some extra bones for you so you can make a large batch and freeze it. Then, invite him for supper to taste your efforts at the stockpot.

The technique for making stock is essentially the same for chicken, beef or lamb bones: by gently simmering bones, vegetables and aromatics together you first extract the flavours. This is followed by a further reduction of the resulting liquid to intensify the flavours.

Stocks are the building blocks of flavour in the kitchen, and are the foundation of good gravy, sauces and soups.

OK, making stock *is* time-consuming – but you don't need to be at the stove for hours: just in your house. Leave a saucepan gently simmering on the lowest possible heat for as long as possible. I would recommend that a minimum of 5 hours would be best. Stock can be made on one of those days when you intend to spend the day at home – you might be spring cleaning; catching up on the ironing or letter-writing; pottering in the garden...

Fresh stock will produce the tastiest gravy. I'm going to resist calling it a jus – that's just too cheffy. From knee-high to a grasshopper, I was brought up on gravy: good, old-fashioned, finger-licking gravy. And that's exactly what it is.

Sauces and soups: light is best

In just the same way that those old-fashioned thickened gravies of yesteryear are way, way out, I've had a big rethink on sauces, too. For years now, my emphasis has been on producing full-flavoured, but essentially light, sauces. In essence that means less cream and more stock, altogether a lighter style of cooking.

Remember, sauces are there to enhance the flavours of the dish, not to mask them. You make or break your starter or main course by the quality of the sauce: if it is too strong it overpowers the dish, too weak and insipid, it will not add to the taste experience of the main ingredients. In my opinion, too many chefs have tended to over-reduce sauces and end up with far too intense flavours. I always say gentle, gentle, gentle.

Dark Stocks

Depending on the desired

flavour, i.e. beef, lamb or

chicken

2 kg (4 lbs 8 oz) beef bones,

preferably marrow bones, and

450 g (1 lb) beef skirt,

trimmed of fat

or

2 kg (4 lbs 8 oz) lamb bones

or

2 kg (4 lbs 8 oz) chicken

carcasses

2 medium onions, chopped and

not peeled

2 carrots, roughly chopped, not

peeled

¼ head celery, chopped

2 leeks, sliced

½ garlic bulb

570 ml (1 pint) red wine

sprigs of rosemary and thyme

good handful of parsley,

including stalks

Method

Pre-heat the oven to 200C/400F/Gas 6. In a roasting tin, firstly brown, but don't burn, the bones in the hot oven (*see* photo 1). This takes about 30 minutes. Then remove the browned bones and place in a very large pan. In the roasting tin in which you browned the bones, saute and colour the onions, carrots, celery, leeks and garlic over a low heat (photo 2). Transfer the vegetables to the pan of bones using a slotted spoon, leaving behind as much fat as possible. Carefully pour this fat into a bowl for roasting potatoes. Over a low heat, deglaze the tin in which the bones have been cooked by pouring in the red wine and, using a wooden spoon, thoroughly scrape the bottom of the tin. Pour the red wine and scrapings into the large saucepan with the bones and vegetables, add the sprigs of rosemary, thyme and parsley and enough water to just cover. When making a dark chicken stock, before covering the bones with water (photo 3), I always sprinkle over a generous heaped tablespoon of brown sugar and three tablespoons of red wine vinegar to give a sweet flavour, which goes well with poultry.

Bring the bones and liquid slowly to the boil, skimming off any scum with a ladle. Simmer very gently to the point where just the occasional bubble can be seen in the liquid, for as long as possible, ideally for at least 5 hours. Strain the stock through a sieve into another large saucepan (photo 4).

This next step allows you to make a really flavoursome-based gravy. In the large saucepan, rapidly boil the stock, removing any scum which may still rise to the surface, so that it reduces in quantity by about half. This will start to concentrate the flavour, but it is essential that you keep tasting the stock, as it reduces, until it reaches the required intensity of flavour. If you prefer a stronger, more intense gravy, you can even reduce it by up to two-thirds. When the flavour of the gravy is to your liking (photo 5, the finished gravy), remove from the heat and pour through a fine sieve into a bowl. Cool, and place in the fridge. Any remaining fat will rise to the surface when the liquid cools, and so can easily be removed. This wonderful intensely flavoured gravy can now be used immediately, stored in a cold fridge for a week, or frozen in small quantities for use at a later date.

My favourite way of using beef gravy in our kitchen is to add some finely chopped shallots, which have been fried in a little olive oil, to a small quantity of the gravy in order to produce a wonderful rich onion gravy. Great with roast beef or calves liver.

Fish Stock

1 onion, peeled and chopped

1 fennel bulb, chopped

1 leek, chopped

2 sticks celery, chopped

10 g (½ oz) butter

1.35 kg (3 lbs) white fish frames
   such as turbot, halibut or sole

275 ml (½ pint) white wine

bouquet garni made up of

   parsley, tarragon and dill

1 lemon, cut into wedges

Method

Gently sweat the vegetables in the butter in a large saucepan so they are soft but not browned. Add the fish frames and the white wine. Top up with 1.7 litres (3 pints) cold water and bring gently to the boil, skimming off any scum that rises to the surface. Add the bouquet garni and the lemon wedges and then simmer gently for no longer than 20 minutes. Strain through a fine sieve.

The fresh stock will keep in the fridge for up to 3 days. It also freezes well.

This stock is a sound basis for fish soups, fish risottos and deliciously tasty sauces to serve with fish.

Vegetable Stock or Nage

2 medium onions, peeled and
   chopped

1 leek, chopped

2 sticks celery, chopped

4 carrots, chopped

whole bulb garlic, cut in half

a handful of fresh herbs,

   tarragon, parsley, dill,

   coriander and chervil

275 ml (½ pint) white wine

1 tbsp peppercorns

1 lemon, chopped into 6 wedges

2.5 cm (1 x 1 inch) lobe fresh

   ginger, chopped

Method

Place all the vegetables and garlic into a large saucepan, add enough water to just cover the vegetables and bring to the boil. Simmer for about 10 minutes. Take off the heat and add the herbs, wine, peppercorns, lemon and ginger. Return to the heat, and simmer for a further 10 minutes. Turn off and allow the flavours to infuse together for 20 minutes. The vegetable stock must then be strained and allowed to cool. It will keep in the fridge for up to 5 days. It also freezes well.

This stock is essential for light sauces that are full of flavour.

White Chicken Stock

1 large onion, peeled and
  chopped

1 large carrot, peeled and
  chopped

1 stalk of celery, chopped

½ bulb of fennel, chopped

2 cloves of garlic, peeled and
  crushed

a splash of vegetable oil

1 kg (2.2 lb) uncooked chicken
  bones

1 large glass of white wine

a few sprigs of parsley,
  tarragon, dill and chervil

Method

In a large saucepan, gently fry the onion, carrot, celery, fennel and garlic in a splash of vegetable oil until they start to soften but without colouring them. Add the chicken bones, wine and herbs and enough water to cover. Bring to the boil, and skim off any scum that forms on the top. Turn the heat down and simmer very gently for a maximum of three hours.

Strain through a fine sieve. The stock is now ready to use.

If you prefer a stronger flavour, return the stock to the heat and reduce by boiling until you have the desired intensity of flavour. In the Morston Hall kitchen, I keep this chicken stock light, as it is the backbone of many of our soups and risottos, and therefore I prefer not to have too strong a chicken flavour coming through.

Allow to cool before storing in the fridge for up to 4 days. Or freeze for use at a later date.

Basil Sauce (see photo 1, page 50)

25 g (1 oz) Dijon mustard

1 tbsp balsamic vinegar

175 ml (6 fl oz) extra virgin

olive oil

40 g (1½ oz) fresh basil

25 g (1 oz) chervil

2 cloves of garlic, peeled and

chopped

20 g (¾ oz) pickled capers, well

rinsed

salt and pepper

Method

Blend the mustard and vinegar in a food processor and, with the machine on high speed, slowly pour in the olive oil followed by the basil, including the stalks, the chervil, garlic and the capers. Process well to create a deep green, rich sauce.

Check the seasoning, and adjust the consistency if necessary by adding a little extra olive oil if the sauce is too thick. The sauce will keep in the fridge for up to five days.

Serve with fillet of beef or spring lamb, and it also works extremely well with fish, if used in moderation.

Beurre Blanc (see photo 2, page 50)

Serves 6–8

2 shallots

1 tbsp wine vinegar

2 tbsp lemon juice

4 tbsp white wine

1 tbsp cold water

225 g (8 oz) salted butter, cut

into cubes

chopped fresh herbs as required

Method

Peel and finely slice the shallots. Place in a saucepan together with the wine vinegar, lemon juice and white wine. Bring to the boil and reduce the liquid to about a tablespoon. Add the cold water, and keep on the heat in order to reduce once again to 1 tablespoon.

Turn the heat down and, over a low heat, slowly whisk in the butter, about 25 g (1 oz) at a time. The sauce will emulsify (thicken and lighten in colour). Once all the butter has been added, remove the pan from the heat and, finally, to complete the recipe, pass the sauce through a sieve into another saucepan. Do not keep the sauce in the fridge as it will separate. To reheat carefully stir the sauce in a saucepan over a low heat.

Then, when you are ready to serve it, stir in some chopped tarragon, chives or parsley, selecting the flavours and quantities according to what you plan as the accompaniments.

Fennel and Mushroom Duxelle

(*see photo 3, page 50*)

1 large fennel bulb, roughly

chopped

350 g (12 oz) field mushrooms,

roughly chopped

1 medium onion, peeled and

roughly chopped

50 g (2 oz) salted butter

salt and pepper

150 ml (¼ pint) red wine

275 ml (½ pint) double cream

Method

Place the fennel, mushrooms and chopped onion in a food processor and blend to a paste.

Melt the butter in a saucepan. Then add the mushroom mixture and cook gently, stirring occasionally, until all the liquid from the mushrooms has evaporated. Season. Stir in the wine and cream, and continue cooking over a moderate heat. Stir occasionally until the liquid has reduced and has been absorbed. The end result should be a fairly thick, but slightly sloppy, sauce.

The sauce can be made in advance – either store in the fridge for up to 2 days, or freeze in an airtight container.

Hollandaise Sauce (*see photo 4, page 50*)

Serves 6–8

3 egg yolks

pinch of salt

½ tsp caster sugar

1 tbsp white wine vinegar

1 tbsp lemon juice

1 tbsp white wine

175 g (6 oz) butter

Method

Place the egg yolks, salt and sugar in a food processor.

Heat the wine vinegar, lemon juice and white wine in a small saucepan, and reduce by half.

In another small saucepan melt the butter and allow to bubble, taking care not to burn it.

Set the food processor to high speed, and pour in the warm, reduced, wine vinegar liquid, followed by the hot melted butter, which should be added very slowly. That's all there is to it: an easy classic hollandaise sauce, which is great with everything from fresh asparagus to grilled fish.

You can make the hollandaise an hour or so before use. All you need to do is leave the sauce in the machine and immediately before serving whizz it up again. If the sauce becomes too thick, simply add a couple of tablespoons of boiling water while the machine is still running.

Tartare Sauce (see photo 5, page 50)

3 egg yolks

pinch each of salt, sugar, English

   mustard powder, black pepper

150 ml (¼ pint) sunflower oil

150 ml (¼ pint) olive oil

1 tbsp white wine vinegar

1 tbsp lemon juice

2 small shallots, chopped finely

2 tbsp flat-leaf parsley, chopped

1 tbsp fresh tarragon

6 small cornichons or 1 gherkin,

   finely diced

We've all had tartare sauce squeezed from a plastic sachet on our fish and chips. But I guarantee you'll enjoy them even more with a dollop of fresh home-made tartare sauce. This recipe is the business.

Method

Place the egg yolks, salt, sugar, mustard powder and pepper in a bowl and, using an electric hand whisk on high speed, beat thoroughly. Next slowly drizzle in the sunflower oil, followed by the olive oil and white wine vinegar. Turn the whisk off and stir in the lemon juice and the rest of the ingredients and mix well. Check the seasoning: I prefer flakes of Malden sea salt and coarsely ground black pepper.

Tomato Butter Sauce (see photo 6, page 50)

450 g (1 lb) vine-ripened

   tomatoes

75 g (3 oz) unsalted butter

1 tsp caster sugar

salt and pepper

My favourite summertime sauce is best made when English tomatoes are in the shops or, better still, when those in your garden are ripe. To make a really flavoursome sauce be certain to use sun-ripened tomatoes with plenty of colour and flavour. If you are wondering why you need to deseed half the tomatoes, when they are in fact all to be sieved, the reason is simple: tomato seeds are full of water and if you leave them all in you'll end up with a watery sauce, lacking in flavour. Do make the sauce a day in advance, but omit the butter until reheating. A must with Chicken and Roquefort Mousse (see recipe, page 67).

Method

Take half of the tomatoes, quarter them, remove the seeds and put in the liquidiser. Now add the remaining tomatoes, which have also been quartered, but this time do not remove the seeds. Blend thoroughly. Push the pureed tomatoes through a fine sieve. To serve the sauce, warm in a saucepan over a low heat, whisk in the butter, add the sugar, and season to taste.

Asparagus Soup

Serves 8–10

3 large bunches Norfolk

asparagus

110 g (4 oz) salted butter

1 large onion, peeled and thinly

sliced

1 small potato, peeled and

thinly sliced

1.2 litres (2 pints) white chicken

or vegetable stock

175 g (6 oz) spinach leaves

150 ml (¼ pint) double cream

salt and pepper to taste

I hate wasting food. Quite simply, this recipe grew out of my dislike of putting an enormous pile of trimmings and stalks on to the compost heap. You might not have such a mass of trimmings, but in May and June when Norfolk asparagus is in season, this recipe is a wonderful way to enjoy a great local delicacy.

Method

Cut the asparagus tips off so they are about the length of your middle finger. Lightly peel the bottom 2.5 cm (1 inch) towards the cut end to create a neat white stalk and a plump green top. Retain the peelings. Put the tips to one side as they can be used in other dishes, such as the Norfolk Asparagus with Rosti Potatoes, Streaky Bacon and Hollandaise (*see* recipe, page 71). Chop the stalks and add to the peelings.

In a large pan, melt half the butter over a medium heat, then add the sliced onion and potato. In another saucepan heat the stock. Once the onions and potatoes are soft, add the asparagus stalks and trimmings, and pour in the hot stock. Bring to the boil and simmer until the stalks are tender.

Take off the heat, add the spinach and whizz up in a liquidiser or food processor. Finally, push through a fine sieve: the easiest way to do this, I find, is with the back of a ladle.

Just before serving, bring the soup back up to temperature, add the remaining 55 g (2 oz) butter and the cream, and check the seasoning.

Serve topped with some blanched, buttered asparagus tips and a thin strip of crispy streaky bacon.

Mussel Soup

Serves 6

1½ kg (3½ lbs) fresh mussels

150 g (5 oz) onions

150 g (5 oz) leeks

110 g (4 oz) carrots

½ fennel bulb

75 g (3 oz) butter

1 clove of garlic, finely chopped

glass of white wine

150 g (5 oz) tomatoes, chopped

700 ml (1¼ pints) fish or

  vegetable stock

1 bouquet garni of thyme,

  parsley, rosemary, tarragon

  sprigs tied together

275 ml (½ pint) double cream

pinch of saffron

salt and pepper

Mussels are one of the many gems of the North Norfolk coast, and we are fortunate to have the finest on our doorstep. However, you must be vigilant when preparing fresh mussels and throw away any that are damaged or do not open when cooked.

Method

Wash and scrape the mussels until they are really clean, making sure that all barnacles and beards are removed. Rinse thoroughly in cold running water for a couple of minutes.

Peel, wash and finely slice the onions, leeks, carrots and fennel into a bowl. Heat half the butter in a large saucepan, and over a low heat sweat a third of the vegetables with the garlic. Turn up the heat, add the mussels and white wine, and place a tight fitting lid on the saucepan. Shake the pan vigorously over the high heat.

The mussels will open when cooked but be sure to discard any that do not open fully. Place a large sieve over a bowl and drain the mussels, retaining the cooking liquor. Next strain this liquor through a fine sieve into another bowl.

Take the mussels out of their shells and set aside, discarding the shells. Melt the rest of the butter in another large saucepan and sweat the remaining two-thirds of vegetables along with the chopped tomatoes, until they are soft but without colouring them. Pour over the fish or vegetable stock, the retained mussel liquor and the bouquet garni, and bring to the boil. Add the mussels, keeping back 12 for garnishing and simmer for about 20 minutes.

Remove the bouquet garni, add the double cream and saffron, and heat to the point where the liquid starts bubbling. Then pour into a liquidiser or food processor, and whizz together thoroughly before pushing through a fine sieve.

When you are ready to serve the soup, bring it back to temperature in a saucepan. Heat the 12 retained mussels in a frying pan with a little oil. Check the seasoning and serve the soup garnished with the mussels.

Roasted Butternut Squash and Parmesan Soup

Serves 8

450–700 g (1 lb–1½ lbs)

  butternut squash

75 ml (3 fl oz) olive oil

50 g (2 oz) salted butter

1 medium onion, peeled and

  finely sliced

1 clove of garlic, crushed

1.75 litres (3 pints) white chick-

  en stock or vegetable stock

275 ml (½ pint) single cream

175 g (6 oz) fresh Parmesan,

  grated

salt and pepper

Harry, our eldest son, was not impressed when I brought home a butternut squash at Halloween instead of a pumpkin for him to carve a face in. The butternut squash was discarded with disdain. I took it to work the next morning and that is how this unique-flavoured soup with its amazing burnt orange colour came about. Perhaps I should call it 'Harry's soup'.

Method

Pre-heat the oven to 200C/400F/Gas 6.

Peel the butternut squash, remove the seeds and cut into small cubes. Place on a roasting tray, and drizzle with the olive oil. Season and place in the oven for 20–25 minutes until the squash softens and starts to brown.

Meanwhile, in a large saucepan, melt the butter and cook the onions and garlic until they soften. Add the stock and bring to the boil. Next, add the roasted squash and single cream. Bring gently back to the boil, simmer for 20 minutes and then whizz in a liquidiser or food processor. Finally, push the soup through a fine sieve.

To serve, gently reheat without boiling, stir in the Parmesan, and adjust the seasoning. Pour into bowls as soon as the cheese has melted. If you plan to serve the soup at a later point, remember not to stir in the Parmesan until you are reheating the soup.

Smoked Haddock and Salmon Chowder

Serves 6

1 medium onion or 2 shallots,

finely sliced

2 cloves of garlic, crushed

½ fennel bulb, diced

olive oil

425 ml (¾ pint) fish or

vegetable stock

1 bouquet garni, made with

thyme, parsley and coriander

225 g (8 oz) small new potatoes,

scraped and quartered

350 g (12 oz) fillet of undyed

smoked haddock, all bones

removed

275 ml (½ pint) milk for

poaching haddock

225 g (8 oz) salmon fillet,

skinned and all pin bones

removed

1 large red chilli, finely chopped

pinch of saffron strands

275 ml (½ pint) double cream

3 tbsp coriander, chopped

225 g (8 oz) baby spinach

leaves, washed

salt and pepper

This recipe always goes down a treat with the fellas on cookery demos. We make it with locally smoked haddock from Cley, and Scottish salmon. It can be made in advance, but be sure not to add the chopped coriander or spinach until just before serving otherwise they'll lose their colour.

Method

Saute the onion, garlic and fennel in 6 tablespoons of olive oil until they just start to colour and soften. Add the fish stock together with the bouquet garni and the new potatoes. Bring to the boil and simmer gently until the potatoes are just cooked. While the potatoes are cooking, lightly poach the haddock in milk, to the point that the flesh just pulls away from the skin. Flake into chunky pieces, checking thoroughly that there are no bones, and put into a bowl. Strain and reserve the milk in which the haddock was poached.

Heat 2 tablespoons of olive oil in a frying pan and gently colour the salmon on both sides, ensuring that it is still pink in the middle. Flake the salmon, and add to the bowl with the haddock.

Once the potatoes have cooked, add the haddock and salmon, along with the finely chopped chilli, saffron, double cream and the reserved poaching milk. Bring back to a simmer and check the seasoning. Just before serving, stir in the chopped coriander and the baby spinach which needs just seconds to wilt. Serve with crusty bread.

Starters

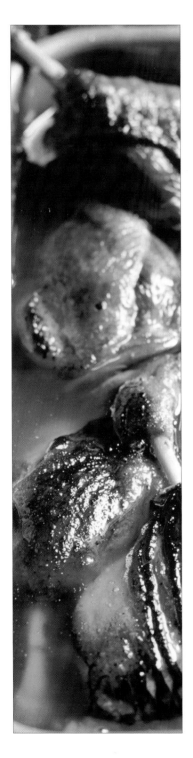

When we opened Morston Hall, we were extremely glad of all the support and input that we received from friends in the locality, our family and industry colleagues. One particular piece of advice though has stuck in my mind: 'always pile the plates high and give them lots of it. That'll be the only way to succeed in Norfolk.'

We listened anxiously, and wondered whether these words could possibly ring true: the 'pile it high, sell it cheap' approach to dining is not really our style. Thankfully we found this to be the case in North Norfolk too.

Small really is beautiful, especially when it comes to starters. What we don't want to do is ruin the appetites of everyone in the dining room at Morston by serving an over-sized dish at the start of the meal. Neither will you want to spoil the chances of your guests enjoying their main course at your dinner party. So go lightly on the quantity of the starter you are planning on serving. Even in the early days at Morston, we never piled on food for food's sake. Now it makes me feel good in the knowledge that guests appreciate dining with us because of our cooking, rather than the amount of food we serve.

The first courses that come out of the kitchen at Morston are carefully planned so that they are not only visually eye catching, but always packed with flavour. After all, they set the scene for the rest of the meal.

I tell everyone in the kitchen that starters must whet the appetite for what is to follow. The same holds true if you are preparing a dinner party menu at home. Remember too that the flavour of any starter dish should not be so intense as to mask the next course.

What's for starters?

So how do we plan a menu, and decide what dish to serve first off? Whether it is for the restaurant or for a meal at home, I always decide – and would recommend that you do too – on the main course first. Then, the rest of the menu can be fitted in, or carefully adapted around it.

Planning a menu is kind of like doing a jigsaw puzzle: you'll need all of the pieces. First, texture: you don't want too many creamy sauces. When it comes to temperature, you don't want all the courses to be hot dishes. Then think about the colour of the ingredients too – aim to give variation through the meal.

The seasons also play an important role for cooks. Ingredients that are in season will be tastier and better value than, say, strawberries grown in the southern hemisphere and imported at Christmas time. In spring there is an abundance of home-grown asparagus – so put it to good use on your menu.

Summer calls for cold starters, terrines and salads. All of these are dishes that can be made in advance, giving you more time with your dinner guests. Autumn sees the start of the game season: think wonderfully rich meat and sauces. Winter menus suit warm starters such as fresh soups, pastas and raviolis.

Remember, if you plan to cook a complicated main course, make it easier for yourself by choosing a simpler starter, perhaps a cold dish that can be prepared in advance.

Last, but not least, your menu needs to fit in with your personal limitations both in terms of the time you can commit to preparing the meal and how confident you're feeling.

Being flexible

All the recipes that appear in this chapter can be developed into light lunches or main courses in their own right. Just increase the amount that goes onto everyone's plate and serve with crusty bread. Another thought: don't be frightened to serve two starters, perhaps one of fish, for a dinner party. Add a salad course, cheese board and pudding, and I guarantee there will be more than enough to go round.

Starters are the first inkling that diners have of your food, so they are not 'something to simply be got through before the main course': they are an integral part of the whole meal experience. For the home cook, again I say 'keep it simple' – let the quality of your ingredients speak for themselves. And if you remember that getting the correct balance of the meal is paramount, your guests will leave feeling warmly satisfied and not bloated. Mission accomplished.

Chicken and Roquefort Mousse

This is probably one of our most talked about starters at Morston because the dish is extremely light yet very flavoursome. If you do not like Roquefort, use any blue veined cheese such as Stilton or Lanark Blue. If you are making this for the first time, I recommend you make a small extra parcel to test that the mousse is perfectly cooked. To prepare ahead, make up the mixture a day in advance and then steam when required.

Serves 8

350 g (12 oz) chicken breast

  with skin removed, diced

1 egg white

425 ml (¾ pint) double cream

110 g (4 oz) Roquefort, Stilton

  or Lanark Blue cheese, broken

  into thumbnail-sized pieces

pepper

Method

Puree the chicken breast meat in a food processor. With a spatula push the mixture back towards the blades, add the egg white and process again.

Remove the puréed chicken from the food processor and push through a sieve into a bowl – this is best done a little at a time with the back of a ladle. Don't use too fine a sieve or you will be at it all day.

Slowly pour the double cream into the chicken mixture, beating carefully with a spatula to reach a dropping consistency. Fold in the pieces of Roquefort cheese, and season with freshly ground pepper.

Lay out eight pieces of clingfilm, about 25 cm (10 inches) square, on a flat surface and, using a large spoon, divide the mousse mixture evenly into the centre of each square (*see* top photo). Bring the 4 corners of each piece of clingfilm together, wrap up tightly and tie a knot as close to the mousse as possible, making a tight ball (*see* middle photo). Use any surplus mousse to make a small spare for testing. Refrigerate until needed.

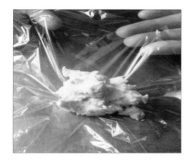

When ready to cook (*see* bottom photo), take the clingfilm-wrapped balls out of the fridge, place in a steamer and steam gently for about 20 minutes until reasonably firm to the touch.

Remove from the steamer and, with scissors, cut the clingfilm to release the mousse into the centre of a serving plate. For maximum taste and visual impact serve with Tomato Butter Sauce (*see* recipe, page 53) and sauteed spinach.

Note: Always remember to use cold water when washing the sieve that has been used for the raw chicken. If you use hot water, you will cook the chicken, making it virtually impossible to remove from the mesh.

Confit of Duck

Serves 4

4 large duck legs

2 cloves of garlic, peeled and
  chopped

4 sprigs of thyme

2 bay leaves

15 g (½ oz) sea salt

freshly ground black pepper

1.5 litres (2½ pints) duck or
  goose fat, or lard

Do not be put off by the idea of meat being cooked and stored in fat – it is an age-old process that works well: confit actually means to preserve in fat. Once the confit is heated up and the fat is drained off, you are left with melt-in-the-mouth meat and crispy skin. The recipe works equally well with chicken or guinea fowl legs. Serve with a crisp green salad or sauteed potatoes.

Method

Marinate the duck legs for at least 12 hours with the garlic, the sprigs of thyme, bay leaves, a generous pinch of salt and a good grinding of black pepper. Remove from the marinade and dry off with kitchen paper.

Pre-heat your oven to 150C/300F/Gas 2.

Heat a dry frying pan until hot, press the duck legs into it skin side down, and fry until the skin is well coloured. Turn the legs over and quickly brown the other side. Put the browned duck legs into a roasting tin large enough to hold them in one layer. Now cover completely with the duck or goose fat. It is essential that the legs are fully submerged in the fat.

On the top of the stove bring the fat up to trembling point, cover with foil and very carefully place into the pre-heated oven. Slowly braise the duck legs for about 2 hours until tender. You can test this by carefully lifting one out with a slotted spoon: the meat should easily start to fall away when you press it. When tender, very carefully remove the duck legs from the fat and set onto a trivet or wire rack in a roasting tin.

Strain the cool duck fat through a fine sieve and keep for another dish; it is especially good for roasting potatoes or making more confit.

When you are ready to serve, pre-heat your oven to 220C/425F/Gas 7. Place the roasting tin near the top of the hot oven for about 6 minutes to heat the duck legs right through and crisp the skin. Alternatively you could do this under a pre-heated grill.

If you are planning to preserve the duck legs for several days, then put them into a clean dish, submerge them completely into the cooled and strained fat, cover with clingfilm and place in the fridge.

Norfolk Asparagus with Rosti Potatoes, Streaky Bacon and Hollandaise

Serves 6

3 bunches Norfolk asparagus

salt and pepper

6 rashers smoked streaky bacon,

  thinly sliced

You can't ever get enough fresh Norfolk asparagus: the season is short – from the end of April to the third week of June – so there's little time to grow tired of this wonderful local speciality. There is really nothing to compare with it.

Method

For the Rosti Potatoes (*see* recipe, page 139).

For the Hollandaise Sauce (*see* recipe, page 52).

For the streaky bacon

Pre-heat the oven to 180C/350F/Gas 4.

Lay the rashers of bacon on a baking tray and cook in the oven at the same time as the rosti until crisp. Remove from the oven, set aside and keep warm.

For the asparagus

Cut the asparagus to about the length of your middle finger. Using a potato peeler lightly peel the bottom inch towards the cut end so you produce a white stalk and a plump green top. This all sounds a bit cheffy, I know, but think presentation, presentation. Reserve the trimmings to make asparagus soup.

Blanch the asparagus in a saucepan of boiling salted water for 2 minutes. Drain immediately, and return to the same pan adding a generous knob of butter and seasoning to taste.

To serve, with a sharp knife, cut the warm rosti on a chopping board into 6 equal sized wedges, and place 1 in the centre of each serving plate. Lay a mound of asparagus on top of the rosti, spoon over the hollandaise and finally top with a strip of crisp, streaky bacon. Serve immediately.

Oriental-style Chicken with Guacamole

Serves 6

4 chicken breasts, skin removed

6 spring onions

2 tbsp sesame seeds, toasted

For the marinade

4 tbsp olive oil

2 tbsp sesame oil

juice of a lime or lemon

lobe of fresh ginger, crushed

2 chillies, red or green, finely
  chopped

bunch of coriander, leaves
  removed, roughly chopped

2 tbsp soy sauce

2 tbsp honey

1 tbsp Worcestershire sauce

For the guacamole

2 ripe avocados, skinned and
  chopped

juice of 2 limes

1 clove of garlic, mashed

4 tbsp fresh coriander, chopped

1 red chilli, finely chopped

1 shallot, finely chopped

150 ml (¼ pint) olive oil

splash of Tabasco

coarse salt flakes and pepper

The beauty of this dish is that it can be served either hot or cold. I prefer the combination of warm chicken with cold guacamole, but this is entirely up to you. Equally adjustable is the degree of spiciness and heat from the amount of chilli you use, both in the marinade and the guacamole.

Method

Mix all the marinade ingredients together in a large bowl. Slice the chicken breasts into 1 cm (½ inch) strips, place in the marinade and gently mix. Leave to marinate for at least 1 hour.

While the chicken is marinating, make the guacamole. Place the chopped avocados into a bowl; pour over the lime juice followed by the rest of the ingredients. Mix well, taste and season. If you do not plan to use it straight away, to help prevent the guacamole from discolouring, push clingfilm directly onto the guacamole to exclude the air. Set aside in a cool, dark place until needed.

Pre-heat your oven to 200C/400F/Gas 6.

Once the chicken has marinated, heat a wok or ridged frying pan on top of the stove until hot, and then quickly sear the marinated chicken strips so they are coloured well. Transfer the chicken strips to a baking sheet or roasting tin and cook in the oven for a further 5 minutes. Remove from the oven and season with coarse sea salt flakes and freshly ground black pepper. Sprinkle with the spring onions, sliced on the bias, and toasted sesame seeds and serve with the guacamole.

Risotto Milanese with Wild Mushrooms

Serves 6

4 shallots or 1 large onion,
  peeled and finely chopped

75 g (3 oz) butter

200 g (7 oz) Arborio risotto rice

425 ml (¾ pint) chicken or
  vegetable stock

1 tsp saffron threads, infused in
  1 tbsp boiling water

225 g (8 oz) mixed wild
  mushrooms

100 g (4 oz) Parmesan, freshly
  grated

3 tbsp parsley, finely chopped

a little oil for frying

salt and pepper

I do not claim to be an authority on the subject, but risotto should be served 'all onda', that is to say, on the wave: when you spoon it onto the plate, it should still flow a little. Like all the best things in life, the more you practise the better you become. The same holds true for the art of cooking a risotto.

Method

In a heavy bottomed pan fry the shallots in the butter until soft, but not browned. With the pan still on the heat, add the rice, stirring constantly, until the grains are well coated in butter. Add 400 ml (14 fl oz) of the cold chicken stock together with the saffron. Season, and bring gently to the boil stirring occasionally. Once the pan is boiling evenly, remove from the heat, cover with a tight fitting lid or foil if necessary. It is important that the pan is covered by the lid or the foil to keep in the steam, which completes the cooking of the rice. Set aside for 30 minutes.

About 5 minutes before removing the lid from the rice, heat a little oil in a frying pan and lightly saute the wild mushrooms, season and set aside.

Remove the lid from the rice and taste. The rice should be cooked and slightly sloppy in texture. If it is too thick add the remaining 25 ml (1 fl oz) of stock.

Finally, stir in the grated Parmesan and chopped parsley, spoon into individual serving dishes and top with the sauteed wild mushrooms.

Salad of Rare Beef and Beetroot with Walnut Dressing

Bursting with summer flavours, this is a rather glamorous starter. The recipe may appear slightly complicated at first, but don't be put off: the various components can be prepared in advance and then very easily assembled. Serve alongside a few small new potatoes and, if you're feeling extravagant, shave Parmesan over the top and add a splash or two of good balsamic vinegar.

Serves 8

For the beef fillet

700 g (1½ lbs) fillet beef

dripping or vegetable oil for
*   sealing the fillet*

salt and pepper

3 large raw beetroot, cooked
*   until very soft*

1 x 225 g (8 oz) pack of young
*   salad leaves*

1 pack chervil, washed

10 g (½ oz) fresh coriander

salt and pepper

For the dressing

1 heaped tsp Dijon mustard

pinch of sugar

150 ml (¼ pint) walnut oil

juice of half a lemon

1 tsp honey

50 g (2 oz) peeled walnut
*   halves, chopped*

salt and pepper

Method

Pre-heat your oven to 200C/400F/Gas 6.

For the walnut dressing

In a bowl place the Dijon mustard and sugar, season, then slowly whisk in the walnut oil and lemon juice. Add honey to taste, and finally the peeled walnuts. Taste again and adjust the seasoning if necessary.

Peel the beetroot and slice very thinly. I find the easiest way to do this is with a Japanese mandolin but, if you don't have one, a sharp knife will always suffice. Place in a bowl and pour over some of the walnut dressing.

For the beef fillet

Heat a frying pan, add the dripping or oil and seal the fillet well on all sides. Place the fillet on a trivet and into a roasting tin, then liberally season. Roast in a hot oven for 20 minutes if you prefer meat very rare, or 25 minutes for medium rare. Take out of the oven and allow the beef to rest. Keep warm.

Pick over the salad leaves. Add to a bowl with the washed chervil and coriander leaves. Mix together.

Just prior to serving, make a circle in the centre of each plate by overlapping the thinly sliced beetroot. Pile thin slices of roast beef on top of this, followed by a handful of the salad leaves.

Finally, drizzle over some more of the walnut dressing and maybe add a few garden dug new potatoes.

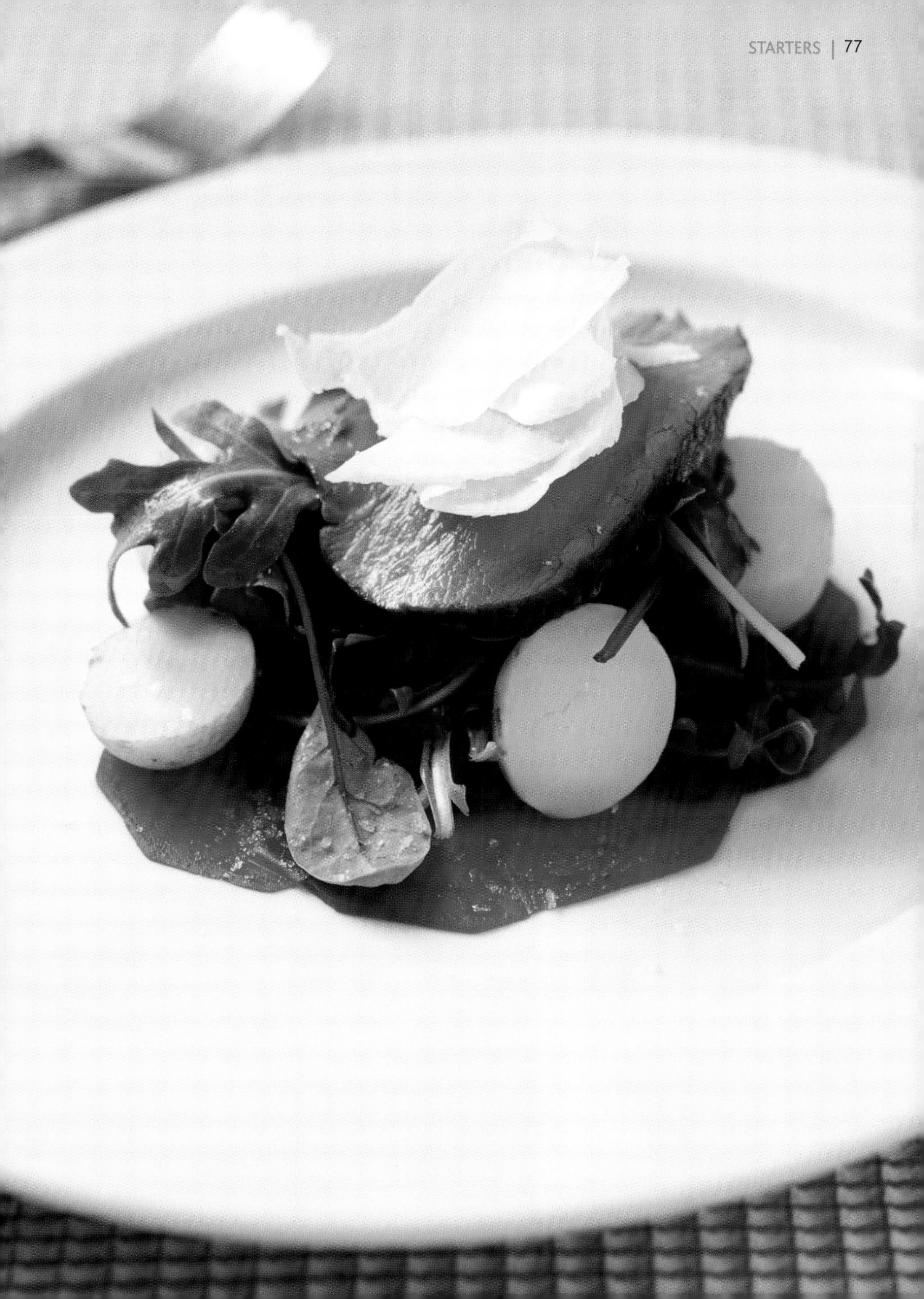

Smoked Haddock Souffle

Serves 10

375 ml (13 fl oz) milk

½ onion, peeled

sprig of thyme

1 bay leaf

225 g (8 oz) undyed smoked
  haddock fillet

275 ml (½ pint) double cream

salt and pepper

75 g (3 oz) salted butter

50 g (2 oz) strong plain flour

pinch of English mustard
  powder

3 egg yolks

6 egg whites

pinch of sugar

2 tbsp parsley, finely chopped

10 ramekins, 7.5 cm (3 inches)

softened butter, for buttering
  the ramekins

Method

Begin by buttering the ramekins well. I always brush them at least twice with softened butter and keep them in the fridge until needed.

Place the milk, onion, thyme and bay leaf into a large saucepan and bring to the boil. Next, add the smoked haddock. Remove from the heat and cover with clingfilm to allow the fish to cook very gently.

In another small saucepan, bring the cream gently to the boil and simmer. Reduce it by half to thicken. Season, and set aside.

When the haddock is just cooked, remove from the milk and flake into a bowl, ensuring that all bones are removed. Strain the milk in which the haddock has been cooked into a jug.

In another saucepan melt the butter over a low heat, stir in the flour and the mustard powder. Cook for 2 minutes, stirring with a wooden spoon.

Pour in the strained milk and beat until the mixture is very smooth and quite thick. Remove from the heat and beat in the 3 egg yolks. Transfer to a large bowl, cover with butter papers or clingfilm and leave to cool.

At least 20 minutes before you plan to serve the souffles, pre-heat your oven to 200C/400F/Gas 6. In a clean bowl whisk the 6 egg whites with an electric hand whisk on a high speed, to the soft peak stage, adding a good pinch of sugar. Using a third of the beaten egg whites, with a slotted spoon beat them quickly into the cooled flour and egg yolk mixture. Next, add the chopped parsley. Then fold the remaining egg whites slowly into the mixture. Be careful not to over work the mixture, as you want it to be as light and airy as possible.

Take the ramekins from the fridge and pour in sufficient seasoned reduced cream to cover the bottom of each dish. Add a layer of smoked haddock, and finally top with the soufflé mixture and level off the top.

Place the ramekins on a baking sheet and bake in the hot oven for about 10 minutes or until the souffles have risen well and are golden brown. Waste no time in serving.

If you want to prepare this dish ahead, poach the haddock and make the base mixture 1 day in advance, and store overnight in the fridge.

Souffles of Mature Cheddar

Serves 8–10

425 ml (¾ pint) milk

slice of onion

pinch of nutmeg

75 g (3 oz) butter

75 g (3 oz) plain flour

pinch of dry English mustard
  powder

250 g (9 oz) strong Cheddar
  cheese, grated

6 eggs, separated

50 g (2 oz) Cheddar cheese,
  finely grated, for finishing

425 ml (¾ pint) double cream

salt and pepper

8–10 ramekins,
  7.5 cm (3 inches)

softened butter, for buttering
  the ramekins

Too many cooks still shy away from making souffles, fearing last minute hassle and disaster. Have no such fears with this recipe: I guarantee it will rise every time and surprise both you and your guests. Being a twice-baked souffle, it can even be frozen and then thawed and cooked. It makes a useful standby for unexpected vegetarian guests too. For the best results, be sure to use a flavoursome Cheddar.

Method

Pre-heat your oven to 190C/375F/Gas 5.

Butter the inside of the ramekins well. Heat the milk with the slice of onion and nutmeg. Bring to the boil and set aside. In a separate pan, melt the butter and stir in the flour and mustard powder. Remove the onion from the milk and bring the milk back to just boiling point. Pour it into the flour mixture and over a low heat continue to beat the mixture thoroughly with a wooden spoon. Remove from the heat and beat in the grated cheese and egg yolks, until the mixture is smooth. Season to taste.

Next, in a clean bowl whisk the egg whites to soft peaks, and fold into the cheese mixture. Fill the ramekins with the mixture until three-quarters full, and stand in a large roasting tin. Pour boiling water halfway up the side of the ramekins and bake in the pre-heated oven for 20 minutes. Once the souffles are well risen, remove from the oven and allow to cool and sink.

Turn the souffles out upside down onto a buttered baking tray. At this point you can store the souffles in the fridge for up to 2 days, or freeze. However, be sure to bring them back to room temperature, or defrost completely before the second cooking.

When you are ready to serve, pre-heat the oven to 200C/400F/Gas 6. Sprinkle the souffles with the extra grated Cheddar cheese, pour over the cream and bake again for about 15 minutes until the souffles are once again well risen and light golden in colour.

Serve the souffles immediately with some of the rich cheese sauce spooned over. A bed of sliced and peeled ripe tomatoes with a liberal sprinkling of snipped chives also makes a good accompaniment.

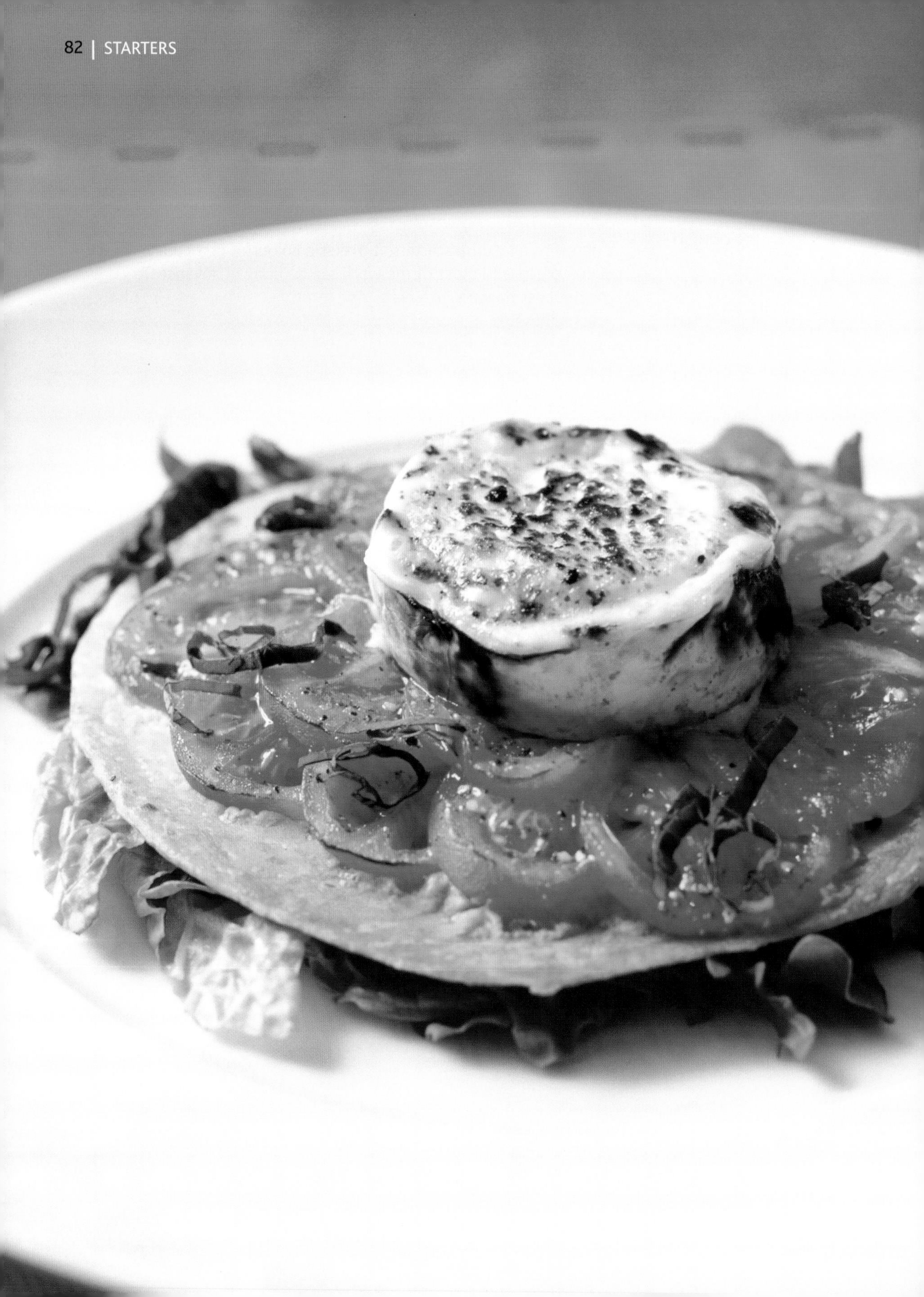

Tomato and Basil Tart with Goats Cheese

One of my favourite starters: it makes a colourful first course for any dinner party, and most of the work can be done in advance. To get the best flavours, use really ripe tomatoes and select a mild goats cheese.

Method

Pre-heat your oven to 200C/400F/Gas 6.

Begin by rolling out the puff pastry as thin as you dare – about 3 mm (⅛ inch) is best.

Using a 9 cm (3½ inch) pastry cutter, cut 6 discs, and place on a greaseproof-covered baking tray. Prick all over with a fork and rest in the fridge for 30 minutes.

Remove from the fridge and cover the pastry discs with another piece of greaseproof paper. Place another baking tray on top of this to weigh the pastry down and prevent it from rising. Bake in the oven for 10 minutes, until the pastry discs are lightly coloured.

Remove from the oven, turn the discs over, cover once again with the greaseproof paper and the baking tray, and return to the oven. Cook until golden. Remove from the oven and leave uncovered on the baking tray to cool. Leave the oven on.

Using a sharp knife, slice the tomatoes very thinly. Using 1 tomato per person, arrange the slices in 6 circles the same size as the pastry discs on a plastic tray.

Season the circles of tomatoes, sprinkle over the basil, give it a light drizzle of olive oil, and finally place the goats cheese on top. Using a wide palette knife or fish slice, put the tomato rings on top of the pastry discs on the baking tray. Return to the hot oven and cook for about 5 minutes or until the cheese just starts to melt.

Remove from the oven, and drizzle lightly with the remaining olive oil. Serve immediately with dressed salad leaves and a sprinkle of really good balsamic vinegar.

Serves 6

225 g (8 oz) Classic Puff Pastry

  (see recipe, page 31)

6 ripe plum tomatoes, blanched

  and skinned

6 large leaves fresh basil,

  chopped

75 ml (3 fl oz) good olive oil

6 small individual soft goats

  cheeses or 6 slices of soft

  goats cheese

1 tbsp balsamic vinegar

salad leaves for serving

sea salt and freshly ground

  black pepper

Fish

After working in a land-locked kitchen for ten years with neither sight nor sound of the sea, let alone a fresh crab, the odd oyster or, God forbid, a live lobster, returning to Norfolk was a dream come true. Having access to the wonderful bounty of the sea, week in, week out, is a real joy. Fresh fish and shellfish are so much a part of being where we are, and why I love being at Morston.

Local fishermen knock on the kitchen door at Morston Hall completely unannounced, laden with fresh fish, caught but a few hours ago. A stone's throw down the road, Mr Bean – the mussel man, who operates the seal boat trips to Blakeney Point – supplies us with the freshest, tastiest mussels known to man. Pop three pound coins into his honesty box on the table outside his house on the main road, just to the west of Morston Hall, and you can take a bag full yourself. Then there's Mr Letzer, who smokes the best salmon in town, and John the fish man from Holt, who consistently comes up trumps with the pick of the day's catch.

We know all these characters personally and that's part of the magic of running a restaurant in a tightly knit village with its heritage in sea life and fishing. The Morston Hall kitchen is not just a number in John's order book – everyone in the kitchen is on first-name terms with him, and our business account is as important to him as his expertise and fresh fish are to us.

Unlike those somewhat spartan days in the north of England, we are not limited to what fish and seafood are available: virtually everything outside our kitchen door is there for the asking and buying.

Norfolk crabs: the very best

Willie Weston supplies us with excellent crabs and lobster. Now I know that many areas along the coast will claim to have the best crabs and that everyone will have heard of Cromer crabs, too, but one of my favourite sources is Blakeney, and this is where you'll find Willie. He really is the fount of all knowledge when it comes to crabs and I've learnt much about this local speciality from him.

May and June are the very best months for really sweet 'full' crab. July is also fairly good but, by the middle of the month, the females – which can be identified by the large apron underneath their body – start shooting their shells as they get bigger. As a result, they lose some of their sweetness.

Not surprisingly, August is the best time for August Jacks. These are male crabs, which you can spot because they have a thin apron, but much larger claws. They are building up for the mating season in September and October, so this is the period when they really are at their prime.

As you can tell by now, fresh crab is a great favourite of mine, which I love serving as an informal luncheon dish if we're entertaining friends, especially if we are dining al fresco. I'll make up a salad plate with some fresh crab, a few cooked English new potatoes, blanched fresh asparagus, a sun-ripened tomato or two, maybe a hard-boiled free-range egg. All that's required then is to drizzle over a little really good olive oil and maybe some well-aged balsamic vinegar. If I really feel like pushing the boat out, I'll add a few fresh shrimps or prawns. Heavenly stuff.

As a youngster, one of my favourite pastimes was to go netting sea bass on the sand bars of the North Norfolk coast. In early summer, the sea bass swim into the warmer, shallow waters of the sand bars to brush their scales in order to rid themselves of the lice. We used to go netting in waders, but I always thought it was best to go barefoot, with our trousers rolled up. This way you could feel the sea bass brushing against your legs, and if you accidentally stood on a dab or a butt it would really make you jump.

Keep it local

North Norfolk offers cooks the freshest fish, so do support your local fishmonger and don't be tempted by all that tropical stuff which is freighted in frozen. The same goes for flabby farmed fish. Remember, too, that brilliantly fresh fish just smells of the sea, it does not give off any fishy smells. This is important to know when buying all varieties of fish, but especially skate.

Fish is quick and easy to cook – so simple, yet so delicious. It is such a wonderful natural product that garnishes are really not called for: always keep it simple. At Morston Hall, fish and seafood come fresh from the North Sea to our kitchen and straight to your table. It's as simple as that.

Cod with Herb Crust on Parsnip Puree

Serves 6

8 slices of stale white bread

1 small handful each of parsley,

chervil, tarragon and dill,

stalks removed

1 clove of garlic, peeled and

crushed

50 g (2 oz) salted butter

6 cod fillets, each weighing

about 110 g (4 oz), skin and

pin bones removed

2 tbsp creamed horseradish

salt and pepper

Not only does the green herb crust look stunning and really compliment the flavour of the fish, but this dish is also perfect for entertaining. It can be prepared in advance, kept in the fridge and then cooked when guests arrive. We are fortunate that John the fish man from Holt is able to get us locally lined cod. Being caught with a fishing line – rather than in a net – means the fish don't get bruised and are therefore of a superior quality.

Method

Begin by making the breadcrumbs. Remove the crusts from the bread and blend in a food processor. Add the herbs and garlic and continue mixing until you have a fine herb crumb mixture, which is a vibrant green. Remove from the food processor and place in a bowl. In the Morston Hall kitchen we push the mixture through a coarse sieve to make absolutely sure that all the stalks are removed.

Next, melt the butter and dip one side of each cod fillet into it. Spread a thin layer of creamed horseradish over the buttered side, and then press this side of the fish into the breadcrumbs. Place onto a buttered baking sheet herb crust uppermost and season.

At this stage the fish can be left in the fridge until you are ready to cook it.

Pre-heat the oven to 190C/375F/Gas 5.

Place the cod into the pre-heated oven and bake for 5 to 10 minutes according to the thickness of the fillets. The fish is cooked once the flesh just starts to flake when pushed with your finger.

You can colour the crumb topping a little more by finishing it under a hot, pre-heated grill. Serve immediately on a bed of Parsnip Puree (*see* recipe, page 139).

Fresh Tuna Nicoise Salad

Serves 6

4 free-range eggs

20 small new potatoes

handful of fine French beans

450 g (1 lb) fresh tuna steak

6 tbsp olive oil

4 Little Gem lettuces

16 black olives, traditionally

  small Nicoise olives should

  be used

1 red onion, peeled and sliced

2 tbsp extra-fine capers

1 small jar of artichoke hearts

6 vine-ripened tomatoes,

  skinned and quartered

6 anchovy fillets, sliced

  lengthways

1 bunch of flat-leaf parsley,

  finely chopped

For the dressing

2 tbsp red wine vinegar

good pinch of sea salt

black pepper

2 cloves of garlic, peeled and

  finely chopped

175 ml (6 fl oz) extra virgin

  olive oil

Essentially a summertime dish, this recipe tastes as good as it looks. Using fresh tuna brings a new dimension to this traditional salad. Preparing all the ingredients in advance gives you a head start and keeps last minute hassle to a minimum.

Method

To make the dressing

Whisk the vinegar, salt, pepper and garlic in a bowl. Continue whisking while pouring in the olive oil. Set aside.

To prepare the salad

First hard-boil the eggs by placing in boiling water for exactly 7 minutes. Immediately cool under cold running water, before peeling and quartering. Set aside.

Cook the new potatoes by boiling in salted water with some fresh mint until tender, drain and set aside to cool.

Top and tail the beans, blanch in boiling salted water. Refresh immediately under cold running water, drain and set aside.

Pre-heat the oven to 200C/400F/Gas 6.

Next, marinate the tuna in a bowl with 6 tablespoons of olive oil. Season and set aside while you prepare the salad.

Break the lettuce into a large serving bowl. Add the potatoes, olives, sliced red onion, capers and artichoke hearts and gently toss together. Add the tomatoes and the quartered eggs, then arrange the anchovies over the top of the salad.

Heat a ridged frying pan on the stove top until hot, and sear the tuna on all sides. Remove from the frying pan and place on a trivet in a roasting tin.

Roast in the pre-heated oven for at least 5 minutes, until the tuna is cooked through. At this point the flesh should just ease apart. Remove the tuna from the oven, slice and arrange on top of the salad.

Finally, whisk the dressing and spoon over the salad as it is served. Sprinkle with sea salt flakes and chopped parsley.

Grilled Lemon Sole with Cream and Parmesan

Serves 4

700 g (1½ lbs) lemon sole,

  skinned and filleted

juice of a large lemon

salt and freshly ground pepper

225 ml (8 fl oz) double cream

1 clove of garlic, peeled and

  finely chopped

2 tbsp parsley, finely chopped

75g (3 oz) fresh Parmesan

  cheese, coarsely grated

This makes a delicious yet simple supper dish, quick and easy to do. When your guests arrive, sit them down and pop the fish under the grill. As an alternative to sole, use plaice, brill, halibut or cod.

It is important that you squeeze the lemon juice over the fish before the cream, to avoid the mixture separating.

Method

Pre-heat the grill to high, or the oven to 200C/400F/Gas 6.

Lay the sole fillets in a buttered gratin dish. The fish should be laid side by side, and not on top of each other, in order that they cook evenly, so be sure to use a dish which is large enough. Sprinkle with lemon juice and season.

Mix the cream, garlic and parsley together in a bowl and pour over the fish. Sprinkle the top with grated Parmesan.

Either cook under the hot grill for 5 to 7 minutes, according to the thickness of the fillets, or near the top of the pre-heated oven for up to 7 minutes. Once cooked, the cheese and cream should form a lovely, bubbly, golden brown topping. Take the dish to the table and serve with crusty bread, new potatoes and fresh, young vegetables.

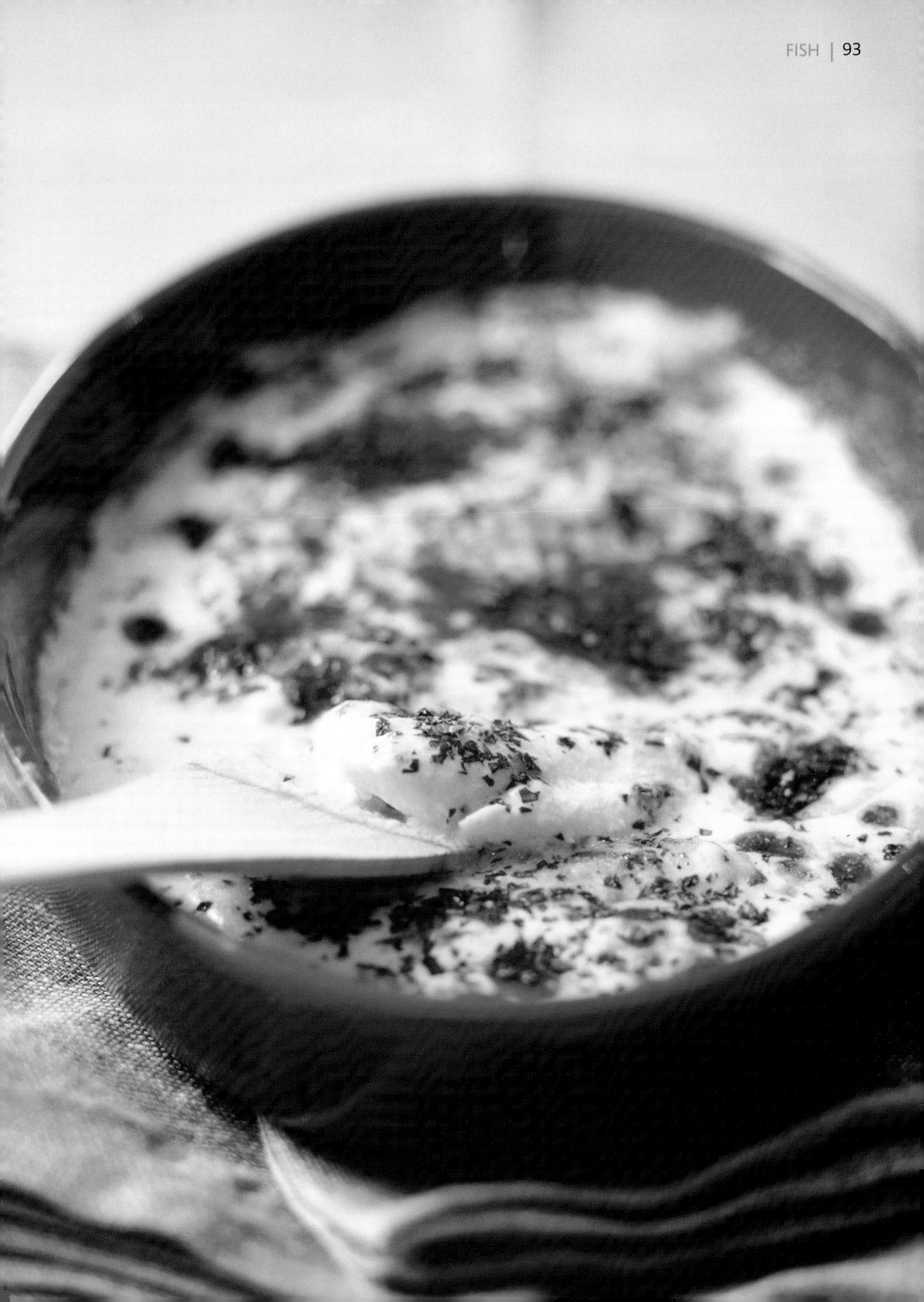

Grilled Sea Bass with Fennel and Mushroom Duxelle

Serves 4

700–900 g (1½–2 lbs) fresh sea

bass, descaled, pin bones

removed and cut into

four fillets

olive oil to brush the skin of the

fish

Fennel and Mushroom Duxelle,

see recipe, page 52

Beurre Blanc, see recipe,

page 51

This is a wonderfully simple way to prepare the freshest sea bass you could ever eat. Truly out of the sea and into the pan.

Method

Pre-heat the grill to high.

Score the skin of the sea bass fillets, being careful not to cut too deeply into the flesh. Season the flesh side of the fish, then arrange, skin side up on a tray and place on the grill pan. Brush the scored skin with olive oil, and place the fillets under the pre-heated grill. Cook for approximately 4 minutes, or until the skin has blackened and the flesh is just cooked.

Serve immediately on a bed of Fennel and Mushroom Duxelle, which has been gently reheated, together with some Beurre Blanc.

Pan-fried Scallops with Guacamole and Crispy Bacon

Serves 4

12 king scallops

2 tbsp olive oil

salt and pepper

6 rashers of smoked streaky

bacon

For Guacamole, see recipe,

page 72 (Oriental-style

Chicken with Guacamole)

Scallops have to rank as one of the foods I most enjoy, but they need to be really fresh. I buy them in the shell, and prefer hand-dived scallops, which are plumper and cleaner than dredged ones.

The rule for scallops is always keep it simple. Before you marinate the scallops, dry them with a clean tea towel, then cook them quickly in a very hot frying pan. That's it.

Overcooking will quickly toughen them: remember, fresh scallops will be cooked once they are just warm in the middle. I tend to cook a spare one for testing – chef's treat!

Method

Firstly, shuck the scallops by carefully easing the shell open with a small, sharp knife. The scallops should come away from the shell with the skirt, muscle and coral. Remove the skirt and the muscle. I also remove the coral, but this is a personal preference. Wash the scallops thoroughly in cold water and pat dry gently with a tea towel.

Place the scallops in a bowl, spoon over the olive oil, season and allow to marinate for 10 minutes.

Pre-heat the grill to hot, and grill the bacon until nicely crisp. Set aside.

Heat a ridged or non-stick frying pan until hot. Over a high heat sear the scallops in the pan for about 2 minutes on each side. The scallops will be warmed, but rare, and if they are fresh this is the best way to serve them. However, if you prefer them done a little more, cook them for just a bit longer on each side. Serve with crispy bacon and a dollop of spicy guacamole.

Pan-fried Smoked Eel on Potato Pancakes with Horseradish Creme Fraiche

Serves 6, makes about 20

pancakes

225 g (8 oz) floury potatoes,

peeled weight

2 tbsp plain flour

2 tbsp milk

1 egg

2 egg whites

1½ tbsp double cream

10 g (½ oz) unsalted butter for

frying the pancakes

a little olive or vegetable oil for

frying the pancakes

250 g (9 oz) full-fat creme

fraiche

juice of half a lime

2 tbsp creamed horseradish or

grated fresh horseradish

275 g (10 oz) smoked eel fillet,

cut into 12 pieces

salt and pepper

These flavours make a great combo. Before you turn up your nose at the smoked eel, though, do try it. Smoked eel has a wonderful flavour and is not as overpowering as you might think. Still not convinced? Smoked salmon fillet makes a good substitute, but I do hope you will try the smoked eel.

Method

Firstly, make the pancakes by peeling and cutting up the potatoes. Boil in a saucepan with a pinch of salt, until the potatoes are soft enough to mash. Drain thoroughly, and return the potatoes to the pan to dry out by shaking over the heat. Push the potatoes through a sieve into a bowl using the back of a ladle or wooden spoon. Beat in 2 tablespoons of flour, 2 tablespoons of milk, 1 whole egg and 2 egg whites, in that order, beating thoroughly between each addition. Cover with clingfilm and set aside for 1 hour before using. Only when you are ready to cook the pancakes, should the double cream be added before mixing thoroughly.

Heat a non-stick frying pan, add a small knob of the butter and a little olive oil and, finally, a tablespoon of the potato mixture. Make several small pancakes at a time in the pan, but be sure to allow plenty of room for them to spread. Cook each pancake for about 2 minutes on each side, until well browned, but still soft in the centre. Remove the pancakes from the frying pan and stack on a plate. They can be warmed up in the oven again when needed. Continue the process until you have used up all the pancake batter.

To make the horseradish creme fraiche, place the creme fraiche into a bowl, and add the lime juice. Season, and then add 2 tablespoons of creamed horseradish or freshly grated fresh horseradish, to taste.

Just before cooking the eel, pre-heat the oven to 200C/400F/Gas 6. Next, heat a non-stick frying pan until hot and, without adding any oil, quickly fry the eel fillets on each side to warm through thoroughly. While the eel is cooking, reheat the pancakes in the pre-heated oven. To serve, place a pancake in the centre of the serving plate, and spoon on a heaped teaspoon of horseradish creme fraiche. Place 1 piece of eel fillet onto the creme fraiche, top this with another pancake, followed by another teaspoon of creme fraiche and another piece of eel fillet. Finally top with a third pancake and sufficient creme fraiche to drizzle elegantly over the stack of pancakes. Serve immediately.

Salad of Morston Crab

Serves 6

4 dressed crabs

2 ripe avocados

juice of 2 limes

1 fresh red chilli, finely chopped

3 tbsp fresh coriander, chopped

150 ml (¼ pint) olive oil

½ bulb of raw celeriac

2 tsp wholegrain mustard

3 tbsp mayonnaise

few drops each of lemon juice,

  Tabasco and Worcestershire

  sauce to taste

salt and pepper

1 x 7.5 cm (3 inch) round

  pastry cutter

Layering the crab with avocado and celeriac may appear to be a bit of a fiddle, but this dish does look stunning, it tastes wonderful and certainly takes crab salad into the 21st century.

The North Norfolk coast, in particular Cromer, is famous for crab. My crab man, Willie, goes out from Morston Quay to pick up his crab pots, and to my mind that makes them the best of all.

Method

Begin by separating the white and dark meat from the crabs, and place in separate bowls.

Peel and chop the avocado into a bowl. Add the lime juice, the chopped chilli and coriander, season and mix well. Stir in the olive oil, cover tightly with clingfilm and set aside.

Coarsely grate the celeriac into another bowl. Stir in the mustard and mayonnaise, and season. If the mixture is too stiff add a little olive oil. This is what is known as remoulade.

Next, season the dark crab meat with a little lemon juice, Tabasco, Worcestershire sauce, salt and pepper, tasting as you do so.

Season the white crab meat with a little lemon juice, salt and pepper and add a drop of olive oil to bind together.

Place a 7.5 cm (3 inch) round pastry cutter in the centre of a serving plate. Spoon a sixth of the dark crab meat into the pastry cutter pressing it down with the back of a spoon. On top of this spoon in a sixth of the avocado mixture, followed by a sixth of the celeriac mixture. Top it off with a sixth of the white crab meat. Press each layer down firmly in turn.

Carefully lift off the pastry cutter to reveal the layered crab salad. Serve with a lightly dressed salad.

Salmon Fish Cakes with Tartare Sauce

Serves 8

6 spring onions, finely sliced

10 g (½ oz butter)

450 g (1 lb) peeled weight of

potatoes, cooked and mashed

1 red chilli, finely chopped

1 tbsp mayonnaise

2 tbsp olive oil

450 g (1 lb) fresh salmon, the

middle fillet is best so the

depth of the salmon is

the same

salt and pepper

4 tbsp parsley or coriander,

chopped

juice of half a lemon

1 egg

75 ml (3 fl oz) milk

110 g (4 oz) white

breadcrumbs

3 tbsp groundnut oil

Method

In a frying pan, quickly cook the spring onions in the butter. Next, add them to the mashed potatoes in a bowl together with the chopped chilli and mayonnaise. Mix well.

Add the olive oil to a non-stick frying pan, and carefully cook the salmon on both sides over a moderate heat for a total of 5 minutes. When I say carefully, I do mean carefully, you don't want to overcook the fish.

Remove from the pan, season and loosely flake into the bowl with the potato mixture. Add the chopped parsley and lemon juice, then gently mix together being careful not to break up the flaked salmon too much. Divide the mixture into 8 portions and, using both hands, carefully but firmly shape each portion into a fish cake.

Make an egg wash by beating together 1 egg and 75 ml (3 fl oz) milk in a bowl. Using a slotted spoon, dip each fish cake into the egg wash before coating well with breadcrumbs. Place the fish cakes on a tray and store in the fridge until you plan to cook them.

When you are ready to serve the fish cakes, pre-heat the oven to 180C/350F/Gas 4. Then heat a non-stick frying pan over a moderate heat, add some groundnut oil and, without crowding the pan, fry the fish cakes for about 2½ minutes on each side until they are well coloured. Keep the salmon cakes warm in the oven until they have all been fried. Serve with dressed salad leaves and home-made Tartare Sauce (*see* recipe, page 53).

Smoked Salmon Mousse with Creme Fraiche, Lime and Dill

Serves 8

For the mousse

275 g (10 oz) Scottish smoked

salmon trimmings

570 ml (1 pint) double cream

juice of one lemon

3 tbsp chives, chopped

3 tbsp cucumber, chopped

a good grinding of black pepper

For the ramekins

1 tsp groundnut oil

225 g (8 oz) smoked salmon,

thinly sliced

For the sauce

200 ml (7 fl oz) full fat creme

fraiche

2 limes cut into segments, skin

and pith removed

10 g (½ oz) fresh dill, finely

chopped, plus 8 small sprigs

for garnish

a little runny honey

salt and freshly ground black

pepper

8 ramekins, 7.5 cm (3 inch)

Method

Roughly chop 275 g (10 oz) of smoked salmon trimmings and blend in a food processor, remember to stop and push down the mixture at regular intervals to ensure all the salmon is well processed. Take the salmon out of the food processor and push a small amount at a time through a large sieve, using the back of a ladle or wooden spoon, into a large bowl. This is quite an effort but is worth it as it will produce a very smooth mousse.

Beat in the double cream, about 150 ml (5 fl oz) at a time, using a spatula rather than a whisk. Continue until all the cream has been incorporated and the mixture is of a dropping consistency. Fold in the lemon juice, chives and cucumber, before seasoning with a good grinding of black pepper. Cover and place in the fridge for 1 hour.

Brush the insides of the ramekins with oil and line the base and the sides with the sliced smoked salmon, leaving an overlap of salmon over the edge of each ramekin. Remove the mousse from the fridge and spoon it into the lined ramekins. Fold the overlapping smoked salmon over the top to cover the mousse. Cover with clingfilm and chill in the fridge. Remove from the fridge 15 minutes before serving.

To make the sauce, stir the creme fraiche in a bowl just to loosen it. Add the lime segments and the chopped dill. Taste, before seasoning and adding a little runny honey to sweeten.

To serve, run a knife round the edge of the ramekin and the smoked salmon lining to loosen the mousse, then turn it out onto a plate smooth side up. Garnish the top with a sprig of dill. Serve with Our Very Popular Wholemeal Bread (*see* recipe, page 23) and lemon-flavoured butter. You can make this quickly and easily by mixing the rind and juice of half a lemon with 50 g (2 oz) soft butter.

The essence of a really top-class, tasty piece of meat always boils down to good provenance – how the animal was raised, and how the meat was subsequently hung and butchered. A good roast joint never came from an inferior piece of meat, and the same holds true for a slow cooked, braised dish such as oxtail or shoulder.

As with all ingredients, but especially with meat, you should always buy the best possible quality you can find. I am a great believer in traditionally produced meats that have been well hung and I am happy to pay a premium for this. These days, though, really good meat does take some searching out.

If I were granted two wishes, I'd probably use them both to improve the quality of the meat we eat. I'll explain…

Firstly, I would wish that all cooks get to know their local butcher. Why? Because, by supporting your butcher, you are shortening the link between what the farmer produces and the ingredients you cook. I believe that this would ultimately mean we would get better quality meat. Buying prepacked meat might be convenient, but we do lose closeness with the land.

It took me nearly five years to develop a sound relationship with our suppliers. Now Morston Hall is well served by a handful of local butchers, each one specialising in something unique to them. Over the years, we've built up a dialogue so they know what the kitchen wants and if the meat is not ready, they won't send it.

Arthur Howell in Binham, our home town, supplies most of our spring lamb and some beef. Another family owned butchers, Rutlands of Melton Constable, also supplies top-notch beef. Then, of course, there's Ray Scoles in Dersingham who sends us ducks and geese. We go out of the county to buy milk-fed lamb from Geoff Sayers in Devon, which becomes available in August.

I'll say it again because it is worth repeating – the source of your meat is of prime importance. More and more guests at Morston want to know where the meat we are serving them comes from. I am more than happy to be able to tell diners exactly which butcher has supplied it and even which farm it was raised on. I do hope my wish comes true and cooks get to know their local butchers.

Secondly, I would wish that farmers could once again start producing meat that is marbled with fat. The trend now might be for beef without fat, but fat equals flavour.

Most beef is too light in colour, which means that it has not been well hung. Hanging develops the richness of flavour of the meat. Sourcing the right quality, good, dark beef with yellowy fat marbled through the flesh is never easy. You will be able to taste the difference though, every time, I do assure you.

Cooking tips

Firstly, never cook meat straight from the fridge. For maximum tenderness, ensure it reaches room temperature before you even think about putting it in the oven.

In a similar vein, in order to keep meat tender once it has cooked, never take it out of the oven and try to carve it straight away. Meat must be allowed time to rest. A chicken will need about five minutes, a joint up to fifteen.

Searing meat in a hot pan before roasting will seal it and help keep it moist during cooking. I also recommend roasting on a trivet as this allows the heat to circulate all around the piece of meat so it cooks evenly.

Knowing when a roast is cooked to your liking will take a little practice. A useful tip, though, is to try what I refer to as 'the hand test'. Touch your thumb with the little finger of the same hand, then feel the pad of muscle at the bottom of your thumb. It will be reasonably taut, and represents meat cooked medium. Now put your index finger and thumb together. The muscle will be much less taut and represents meat cooked very rare.

Finally, it helps to have a well-sharpened knife for carving. You could always ask a favour of your new best friend – your local butcher. After all, he knows a thing or two about knives.

Fillet of Beef

Serves 6

6 x 150 g (5 oz) fillet steaks,

  ideally 2.5 cm (1 inch) thick

25 ml (1 fl oz) olive oil

25 g (¾ oz) salted butter

salt and pepper

Fillet of beef should be well hung, dark in colour, with fat marbled through. It is difficult to find, I know. It is also expensive, but what you see is what you eat and there is no waste. At Morston we serve this dish with either Basil Sauce or Caramelised Port-glazed Shallots (*see recipes, pages 51 and 134 respectively*).

Method

Pre-heat the oven to 220C/425F/Gas 7.

Heat a deep-sided frying pan, and add the olive oil and butter. With the pan still on a high heat, fry the steaks for about 1 minute on each side to seal and colour them.

Remove the steaks from the pan and place on a trivet in a roasting tin, season, then roast in the pre-heated oven for 5 minutes.

Remove from the oven, cover with foil, and allow to rest in a warm place for up to 3 minutes before serving.

Grilled Breast of Guinea Fowl with Lime and Ginger

Serves 6

6 guinea fowl breasts, skin left
  on

2.5 cm (1 inch) lobe fresh
  ginger, peeled and grated

juice and rind of two limes

4 tbsp olive oil

1 tbsp runny honey

1 small knob of salted butter

salt and pepper

I always think of this as a wonderfully refreshing main course with summer in mind. Guinea fowl are now readily available, and make an excellent alternative to chicken. Do be careful though when grilling, as the meat can quickly become dry.

The legs can be used for Confit (*see* recipe, page 68).

Method

In a large bowl marinate the guinea fowl breasts with the ginger, lime, olive oil and honey for up to 4 hours, turning at least once.

Pre-heat the grill. In the meantime, heat a frying pan until hot, add a little butter, allow it to foam and then seal the guinea fowl breasts, skin side down. Once they are well browned, turn over and quickly colour the underside.

Remove the breasts from the frying pan, season and place skin side up on a grill pan. Grill under the pre-heated grill for about 10 minutes. Rest in a warm place for 2 minutes before serving. Good accompaniments include French Beans Lyonnaise (*see* recipe, page 136) and freshly dug new potatoes from the garden.

Loin of Venison en Croute

Serves 4

275 g (10 oz) puff pastry

25 g (1 oz) butter

450 g (1 lb) boned weight loin
   of venison, fat and gristle
   removed

salt and pepper

3 Parsley Pancakes (see recipe,
   page 173)

6 tbsp Fennel and Mushroom
   Duxelle (see recipe, page 52)

1 egg, beaten

In Norfolk, venison is reared in the parks of some of the most beautiful country houses. The venison is pretty good too. We use small loins from fallow deer because they are more tender. As vension tends to be a dry meat, wrapping in Parsley Pancakes plus a short cooking time will ensure it stays succulent.

Method

On a floured surface, roll out the pastry into a rectangle approximately 25 x 30 cm (10 x 12 inches). Place on a baking sheet, cover with clingfilm and put in the fridge to rest.

Heat a frying pan on a high heat, add the butter, and seal the loin of venison, turning it so that it colours all over. Remove from the pan, season and leave to rest and cool completely.

Once you are ready to assemble the dish, take the pastry from the fridge and lay it on a lightly floured surface. Arrange a single layer of the 3 large Parsley Pancakes on top of the pastry, overlapping the pancakes if necessary. Next place 3 tablespoons of duxelle into the centre of the pancakes. Spread this out into a layer, the same size as the loin of venison. Place the venison on top of the duxelle before spreading the remaining duxelle on top of the meat. At this stage you will have a layer of pastry covered with a layer of the 3 Parsley Pancakes, and in the centre of this the venison covered with duxelle, sitting on a layer of duxelle.

You next need to create a parcel where the venison is wrapped in the pancakes, which in turn are encased in pastry. Start by folding the 3 Parsley Pancakes over the loin. Then brush the edges of the pastry with the beaten egg so that you can seal the edges. Next, gently wrap the pastry around the loin. You should end up with a parcel of venison surrounded by a layer of Parsley Pancake, which is encased in pastry. Push any pastry edges tightly together to ensure they are sealed, brushing with more beaten egg if necessary.

Turn the parcel over so that the untidy sealed edges are at the bottom, and set the smooth topped pastry parcel on a greaseproof lined baking sheet. Place in the fridge for at least 30 minutes. Pre-heat the oven to 220C/425F/Gas 7. Remove the venison parcel from the fridge and brush all over with the remaining beaten egg and cook in the oven for 30 minutes until the pastry is golden.

Remove from the oven, and leave to rest in a warm place for at least 5 minutes before slicing and serving.

Marmalade Roasted Breast of Duck

Serves 4

2 whole ducks each weighing

about 2.3 kg (5 lb)

2 tbsp marmalade

salt and pepper

This may seem a very short time to cook duck but because the legs have been removed, this makes a big difference to the cooking time. This recipe will give you breast meat cooked pink, but you can of course roast the duck for longer if you prefer. I recommend cooking the breasts on the bone so that they keep their shape and retain more flavour.

Method

Remove the legs from the ducks leaving the breasts on the carcass. You can use the legs for making Confit of Duck (*see* recipe, page 68).

Pre-heat the oven to 200C/400F/Gas 6. Score the skin on the duck breasts with a sharp knife, being careful not to cut through to the flesh.

Heat a frying pan on the top of the stove, and then seal and brown the ducks all over.

Place the ducks, breast side up, in a roasting tin, season and roast in the pre-heated oven for 30 minutes. Take out and liberally coat with marmalade, return to the oven for a further 15 minutes.

Remove from the oven and rest in a warm place for 10 minutes before carving the breasts off.

Serve with a sauce made from a reduced duck or chicken stock and orange segments added just prior to serving. Boiled new potatoes go well with this dish too, as they counteract the richness of the duck.

Pan-fried Calves Liver

Serves 4

450 g (1 lb) calves liver. Ask

your butcher to cut the liver

into 6 mm (¼ inch slices)

little plain flour

5 ml (2 fl oz) vegetable oil

salt and pepper

Many of us still shy away from eating liver: memories of overcooked, tough, sinewy lambs or pigs liver linger on.

Shake off your preconceived ideas and try calves liver. Mild in flavour and mouthwateringly tender, it's a different dish altogether. Cook, and eat it straight away.

Method

Begin by carefully removing any large arteries and sinews with a small sharp knife, as they can be quite tough and unappetising.

Heat a frying pan and add the vegetable oil. Dust the calves liver in seasoned plain flour, and cook in the hot frying pan for about 2 minutes on each side.

Serve immediately with mashed swede and Onion Marmalade (*see* recipe, page 172).

Roast Breast of Free-range Chicken with Mascarpone

Serves 4

250 g (9 oz) tub of Mascarpone

1 clove of garlic, crushed

1 tbsp each tarragon, chives and

   parsley

juice and rind of half a lemon

4 free range organic chicken

   breasts, skin left on

olive oil for cooking

salt and pepper

The earthiness of lightly sauteed wild mushrooms compliments this highly flavoured chicken dish perfectly. If you're feeling really adventurous, try serving it with Home-made Pasta (*see* recipe, page 40).

Method

In a bowl, mix together the Mascarpone, garlic, herbs, lemon juice and rind. Taste and season.

The next stage will be to put a small layer of the Mascarpone mixture under the skin of the chicken breast.

To do this, first create a small pocket by inserting your index finger between the skin and flesh of the chicken. Move your finger gently from side to side to open up the space under the skin, being careful not to make the hole too big. Then carefully push a quarter of the Mascarpone mixture into this pocket and fold the skin back to close the hole. I find it easier to use a piping bag with a plain nozzle but fingers will do the job just as well if you find piping fiddly.

Place the stuffed chicken breasts on a baking tray and chill in the fridge for at least 1 hour.

Pre-heat the oven to 200C/400F/Gas 6.

Heat a frying pan until hot on the top of the stove, add 1 tablespoon of olive oil and then brown the chicken breasts, skin side down in the hot pan. Turn over and quickly brown the underside. Transfer to a trivet in a roasting tin, place in the pre-heated oven and roast for 25 minutes. Remove from the oven and allow to rest in a warm place before serving.

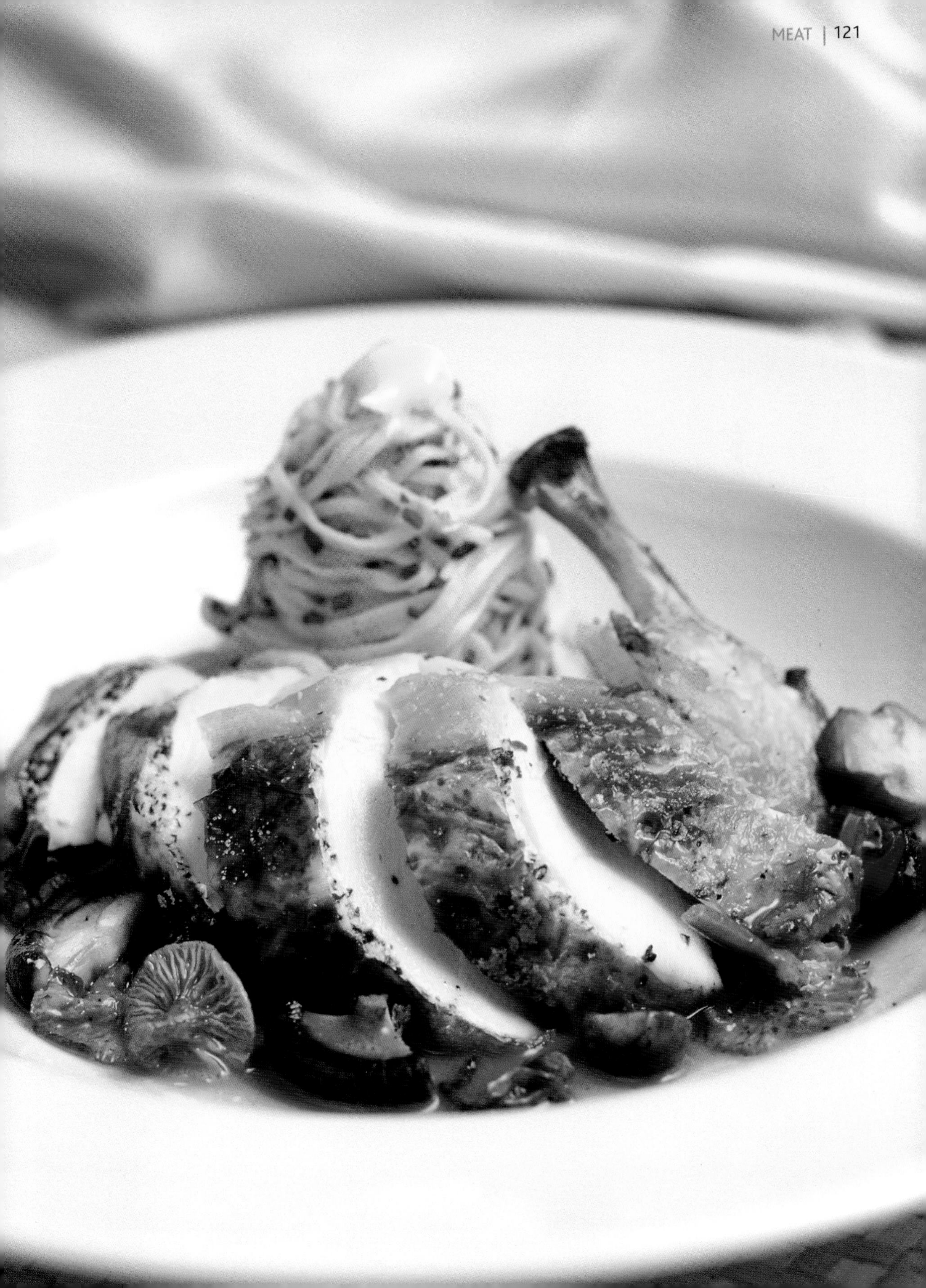

Roast Leg of Spring Lamb, studded with Garlic and Rosemary

Serves 6

1 leg of lamb about 3 kg

(6½ lbs) with the chump left

on – ask your butcher to

remove the aitch bone

4 cloves of garlic

sprigs of rosemary and thyme

50 g (2 oz) butter

50 g (2 oz) redcurrant jelly

sea salt flakes

coarsely ground black pepper

This recipe will give you succulent roast lamb, pink in the centre and well done on the outside. Rustic Ratatouille goes well with this dish, (*see* recipe, page 141).

Method

Pre-heat the oven to 200C/400F/Gas 6.

Using a sharp knife make incisions about 1 inch deep all over the lamb, and insert the garlic, rosemary and thyme. Remember to do the underside as well. Smear the lamb with butter, and season.

Sit the lamb on a trivet in a roasting tin, and place in the pre-heated oven. After 1 hour remove from the oven, coat well with redcurrant jelly, and return to the oven for a further 20 minutes.

Finally, allow the lamb to rest in a warm place for at least 10 minutes before carving.

Roast Rack of Lamb

Serves 4

2 well-trimmed racks of lamb

  (minimum of 6 ribs each) – ask

  your butcher to chine the lamb

  and remove all the back fat

30 ml (1 fl oz) olive oil

25 g (1 oz) butter

salt and pepper

There is nothing quite like the first English spring lamb: my favourite. I never tire of it. The Welsh think their lamb is the best; the Scots do too. I'm biased – give me Norfolk lamb every time.

Ask your butcher to French trim the racks, which means that all the fat should be taken off, the ribs exposed, cleaned, and chined.

Method

Pre-heat the oven to 220C/425F/Gas 7.

Heat a frying pan until hot, then add the oil and butter and allow to foam. Add the lamb, meat side down and seal all over. Next, place the lamb on a trivet in a roasting tin. Season well, and roast in the pre-heated oven for about 20 minutes for pink lamb, or for up to 30 minutes if you prefer your lamb better done.

Remove from the oven and keep warm for 5 minutes to allow the meat to rest before serving. Roasted lamb is always wonderful with Fondant Potatoes, Baked Aubergine (*see* recipes, pages 136 and 133) and rich lamb's gravy.

Roast Rack of Pork with Crackling, Lemon, Garlic and Sage

Serves 6–8

1 rack of pork, about 3 kg (6½

lbs), with at least 6 ribs, which

has been chined and scored

2 cloves of garlic, thinly sliced

rind of a lemon peeled with a

zester

24 leaves of sage

salt

If you want really good crackling look for a dark, dry skin when buying your pork. Some people rub the skin with olive oil, but my tried and tested way is to splash it with cold water and then salt it.

Method

Pre-heat the oven to 220C/425F/Gas 7.

Firstly, weigh the pork and calculate the cooking time according to the weight. You do this by allowing 20 minutes per 450 g (1 lb) of meat, then adding 20 minutes extra.

Next make incisions about 2.5 cm (1 inch) apart through the rind and into the flesh with a sharp knife before pushing the garlic, lemon rind and a sage leaf into each cut. Place the pork in a roasting tin, and splash the rind with cold water before liberally sprinkling with salt.

Place the roasting tin on the top shelf of the pre-heated oven and roast without opening the oven door for 25 minutes. During this time, the crackling should start to bubble.

Turn the oven down to 190C/375F/Gas 5, and continue to roast for the remainder of the calculated cooking time. By now you should have good crackling and moist succulent meat. Check whether the meat is cooked properly with a skewer, the juices should run pink but not bloody. Remove from the oven and allow to rest for 5 minutes in a warm place before carving.

Very Slowly Braised Oxtails

Serves 4

75 g (3 oz) dripping or lard

2 oxtails, jointed and trimmed
  of fat

225 g (8 oz) carrots, chopped

1 large onion, chopped

2 sticks celery, thinly sliced

225 g (8 oz) leeks, sliced

450 g (1 lb) tomatoes, chopped

sprig of thyme

4 cloves of garlic, crushed

275 ml (½ pint) red wine

1.4 litres (2½ pints) beef stock

salt and pepper

Oxtails are always best cooked a day in advance as, like all slow-cooked meats, the flavours will be enhanced. The highlight of the dish is an amazingly rich, sticky gravy which is best eaten with a mound of mashed potato.

Method

Pre-heat the oven to 150C/300F/Gas 2.

Heat a large frying pan over a high heat, add the dripping or lard, and fry the oxtails until browned all over. Remove the oxtails, season and place in a large casserole.

Fry the chopped vegetables in the same frying pan and, once they have started to colour, add the chopped tomatoes, thyme and garlic and continue to cook for a few minutes. Then add these vegetables to the oxtails in the casserole.

Next add 275 ml (½ pint) red wine and sufficient beef stock to cover the oxtails and, over a medium heat, bring to a steady simmer, season and cover. Place the casserole in the pre-heated oven for a minimum of 4 hours, or until the meat is extremely tender. Remove from the oven, and with a slotted spoon transfer the oxtails to a roasting tin, allow to cool and then cover with foil and place in the fridge, preferably overnight. Strain the stock into a large bowl and when cool place this in the fridge overnight as well.

The next day, take off as much fat as possible from the top of the stock. Place the stock in a large saucepan and boil over a high heat for about an hour to reduce the stock by at least half and intensify the flavour, tasting as it reduces.

Half an hour before you are ready to serve, pre-heat the oven to 180C/350F/Gas 4, remove the oxtails from the fridge, take off the foil and place the roasting tin into the oven for about half an hour until the oxtails are heated right through. Finally, serve with plenty of the rich gravy and some mashed potatoes.

Vegetables

Baked Aubergine

Serves 4

2 aubergines

splash of olive oil

2 cloves of garlic, crushed

sprigs of fresh thyme and
   rosemary

salt and pepper

Thank goodness those wonderful plump, purple Italian aubergines are becoming more readily available as, grown outdoors, they have infinitely more flavour. This is an easy dish that is often served with lamb at Morston.

Method

Pre-heat the oven to 150C/300F/Gas 2. Cut the aubergines lengthways and, with a knife, criss-cross through the flesh without breaking the skin.

Cover a baking sheet with aluminium foil, and place the aubergines on it. Drizzle a little olive oil over each half and spread with the garlic. Place some sprigs of thyme and rosemary on top of the garlic, season, and draw up the sides of the foil to make a sealed parcel. Bake in the pre-heated oven for about 1 hour, or until tender and moist. Remove from the oven, scoop out the flesh onto a board, and chop finely. Check the seasoning and serve immediately.

The aubergines can be prepared up to a day in advance and reheated in a saucepan over a low heat.

Braised Fennel with Orange

Serves 4

4 tbsp olive oil

2 fennel bulbs, halved and
   quartered lengthways

4 tbsp tarragon vinegar

2 cloves of garlic, crushed

425 ml (¾ pint) chicken stock

rind and juice of one orange

salt and pepper

As fennel has a strong aniseed flavour, I am never sure if I really enjoy its flavour or not. Then, the first taste of this dish reminds me just how interesting it really is.

Method

Heat the olive oil in a frying pan and, on a high heat, brown the fennel on all sides. Keeping the pan on a high heat, add the tarragon vinegar, crushed garlic and chicken stock. Bring to the boil, season, cover the pan and cook gently for about 30 minutes, until the fennel is tender. Remove the fennel with a slotted spoon and keep hot. Boil the remaining liquid with the orange rind and juice until it is reduced to a sauce consistency. To serve, place the fennel into a dish and pour over the reduced sauce. Ideal with roast duck or game dishes.

Bubble and Squeak

Serves 6

2 large baking potatoes, King
*   Edward or Desiree*

25 ml (1 fl oz) olive oil

225 g (8 oz) swede, peeled and
*   diced*

½ Savoy cabbage, trimmed and
*   destalked*

110 g (4 oz) salted butter

110 g (4 oz) shallots or onion,
*   finely sliced*

1 clove of garlic, crushed

1 tsp thyme, finely chopped

1 tsp parsley, chopped

salt and pepper

This is my way of taking an old favourite for using up yesterday's left overs, into the new millennium.

Method

Pre-heat the oven to 200C/400F/Gas 6. Rub the potatoes with olive oil and bake in the hot oven for about an hour, until cooked.

While the potatoes are baking, prepare the vegetables. Cook the swede in boiling, salted water until soft, and then drain off.

Blanch the cabbage in boiling, salted water, refresh under cold running water and drain. Melt the butter in a large frying pan. Saute the onions, garlic and thyme until lightly coloured, add the cabbage and cook for 2 minutes over a medium heat.

Take the baked potatoes out of the oven and remove the skins.

Finally, mash the boiled swede and baked potatoes together or, alternatively, push through a potato ricer. Add to the pan and combine with the cabbage and onion. Stir in the chopped parsley, and check the seasoning. Serve with hearty meat dishes such as sirloin, rib-eye or fillet of beef.

Caramelised Port-glazed Shallots

Serves 4

900 g (2 lbs) shallots

50 g (2 oz) butter

2 tbsp redcurrant jelly

275 ml (½ pint) port or red wine

salt and pepper

This is essentially an autumn dish for using small shallots at their best. Baby onions will do instead but, whatever you do, don't go and use your best vintage port. Ideal with game or meat dishes.

Method

Peel the shallots and blanch in boiling, salted water. Melt the butter in a large pan, add the shallots, and brown well over a high heat. Add the redcurrant jelly and port, turn the heat down and slowly reduce the liquid. Once it has become syrupy, turn off the heat and season. The shallots should now be cooked and soft.

Reheat when required in a saucepan over a low heat.

Celeriac Mousse

Serves 4

225 g (8 oz) celeriac

50 g (2 oz) salted butter

275 ml (½ pint) double cream

2 eggs

salt and pepper

4 x 7.5 cm (3 inches) well
buttered ramekins

For too long celeriac has been dubbed that knobbly vegetable that no one knows how to cook. Thank goodness that's changing. Add sliced tomatoes and grated Parmesan to this mousse to create an attractive vegetarian dish. Celeriac is also an excellent accompaniment to game.

Method

Pre-heat the oven to 180C/350F/Gas 4

Peel the celeriac and dice into small cubes. Melt the butter in a saucepan and slowly sweat the celeriac until soft. Add the double cream and, keeping on a low heat, stir and allow to thicken slightly. Pour the mixture into a liquidiser, add the eggs, season, and blitz on high speed.

Spoon the celeriac mousse into the prepared ramekins. Place the ramekins in a deep-sided roasting tin, pour in boiling water to a third of the way up the sides of the ramekins, then carefully put into the oven. Cook for 20 minutes until just set, remove from the oven and allow to rest for 5 minutes. Finally turn out the mousses on to a plate.

Serves 6

2 heads of Savoy cabbage

175 g (6 oz) butter

1 tbsp fresh sage, chopped

salt and pepper

Etuvee of Savoy Cabbage

Sounds posh doesn't it? But etuvee simply means 'braised' in French. This recipe will produce the most beautifully soft cabbage, which retains its colour. Yes, the recipe calls for lots of butter, but this is a vegetable dish to die for.

Method

Begin by stripping the cabbage leaves, discarding any damaged outer leaves and removing the central vein. Blanch the leaves in fiercely boiling, salted water for about 4 minutes. Refresh immediately in very cold running water. This will halt the cooking and also retains the colour. Place the leaves on a clean tea towel and pat dry.

Heat a large pan, add the butter and then the cabbage leaves. Cook gently over a low heat until the cabbage becomes very soft. Add the sage, and check the seasoning before serving. This dish is best eaten straight away, but at a push it will keep for a few hours and can be reheated by gently warming through in a saucepan.

Fondant Potatoes

To create a soft centre with a crisp outside – a fondant – you will need good roasting potatoes, such as King Edwards, for this recipe.

Method

Cut two sides off each potato to give you a flat potato about 2.5 cm (1 inch) thick. Then using a 5 cm (2 inch) plain round cutter, cut a disc out of each potato. The disc should look like an ice hockey puck. Keep the trimmings and use them for mash.

Spread the base of a 25 cm (10 inch) non-stick saute or frying pan with all the butter. Lay the potatoes on the butter and season. Completely cover the potatoes with cold water and add the garlic and thyme. Over a high heat, bring to the boil and continue boiling until most of the water and butter has been absorbed by the potatoes. When the potatoes start to colour on the bottom and sides, remove from the heat and allow to stand for about 5 minutes. This will prevent the potatoes sticking to the pan.

Next, turn the potatoes over, return to the stove and continue cooking on a fairly high heat to colour the other side. When coloured, remove from the heat and allow to stand for 5 more minutes before serving.

Serves 4

8 large potatoes, peeled

110 g (4 oz) unsalted butter

½ garlic bulb

some sprigs of thyme

salt and pepper

French Beans Lyonnaise

Method

Blanch the beans briefly in a saucepan of boiling salted water so that they still retain their colour and a little bite. Refresh under cold running water, and drain.

In another saucepan, melt the butter and saute the shallots until soft, without browning them. Add the cold beans, stir gently until warmed through, season and serve.

This makes a good accompaniment to guinea fowl, but can also be served cold dressed with a vinaigrette.

Serves 6

275 g (10 oz) extra-fine French beans, topped and tailed

3 shallots, peeled and finely chopped

25 g (1 oz) butter

salt and pepper

Mashed Swede with Horseradish

Serves 6

450 g (1 lb) swede, peeled and
* roughly chopped*

110 g (4 oz) butter

2 tbsp creamed horseradish

salt and pepper

Swede is an underrated vegetable, but it really comes to life with the addition of a little horseradish.

Method

Place the swede in a large saucepan, cover with cold water and add a generous pinch of salt. Bring to the boil and simmer with the lid on until the swede is very soft. Strain well, and mash.

Add the butter, horseradish and a good grinding of black pepper and mix together well. Alternatively, for a smoother finish, you could process the strained swede, butter and horseradish in a food processor.

Serve immediately or, if preparing ahead, allow to cool and then gently reheat in a saucepan over a low heat when required.

Olive Oil Mashed Potatoes

Serves 6

150 ml (¼ pint) milk

2 cloves of garlic, peeled and
* finely chopped*

2 sprigs fresh thyme

1 sprig rosemary

450 g (1 lb) floury potatoes
* such as Desiree, peeled and*
* chopped*

175 ml (6 fl oz) olive oil

salt and pepper

I first ate this at the Bibendum restaurant in London when Simon Hopkinson was head chef. It really is potato nectar. Great with Very Slowly Braised Oxtails (*see* recipe, page 128).

Method

Pour the milk into a pan, add the garlic, thyme and rosemary and bring to the boil. Turn off the heat, cover, and leave to infuse while you prepare the potatoes.

In a saucepan, cover the potatoes with cold water, add salt, and bring to the boil. Cook until soft, then drain in a colander. Return the potatoes to the saucepan and dry them out by shaking the pan over a low heat. Push the potatoes through a sieve into a bowl. Alternatively, push through a potato ricer. You can also use an electric hand-held beater or mixer for this stage of the recipe. However, you cannot use a food processor as it will make the potatoes too sticky and glutinous.

Strain the milk into another pan, add the olive oil, return to the heat and slowly bring to the boil. Next, vigorously whisk the hot milk and olive oil into the potatoes to create a mixture with a fairly runny consistency. Adjust the consistency by adding more olive oil if required.

Taste, season and either serve immediately or, if preparing ahead, allow to cool and gently reheat by stirring in a saucepan over a low heat.

Potatoes Dauphinoise

This classic potato dish is extremely versatile: you can top it with cheese, but my favourite way of cooking it, particularly for serving with fish or chicken, is to add a little lemon rind. At Morston we use a pastry cutter to make neat, individual portions. At home, though, I'd be much more inclined to take the gratin dish to the table and let guests help themselves.

Method

Pre-heat the oven to 180C/350F/Gas 4.

Slice the potatoes thinly. The best way to do this is with a Japanese mandolin, but do watch your fingers. Place the potatoes in a large bowl with the garlic, cream, lemon rind and a little freshly grated nutmeg. Season, and mix well with your hands.

Spread the potatoes evenly in a buttered oven-proof gratin dish, about 20 x 25 cm (8 x 10 inches) or a deep-sided, buttered, roasting tin.

Cover with greaseproof paper and place in the pre-heated oven for about an hour until the potatoes are cooked completely. Test this by pushing a skewer into the potatoes: they should be soft. Remove the greaseproof paper and cook for a further 20 minutes in order to brown the top of the potatoes.

Remove from the oven and serve. Topped with bacon and cheese this could be a meal on its own. It is also good with duck and most poultry dishes.

Serves 8

900 g (2 lb) potatoes, peeled

2 cloves of garlic, peeled and

crushed

570 ml (1 pint) double cream

rind of a lemon

pinch of freshly grated nutmeg

salt and pepper

butter for greasing gratin dish

Parsnip Puree

Serves 6

*450 g (1 lb) parsnips, peeled
and diced into small pieces*

275 ml (½ pint) single cream

freshly grated nutmeg

salt and pepper

A wonderful accompaniment to Cod with Herb Crust (*see* recipe, page 88), this dish can be made in advance and then gently reheated.

Method

Peel the parsnips and dice into small pieces. Put into a saucepan and cover with cold water. Add a pinch of salt, bring to the boil and simmer until very tender. Drain thoroughly. Blend in a food processor with the cream, season with a little freshly grated nutmeg, salt and pepper. In the kitchen at Morston Hall we then push the parsnips through a sieve to ensure there are no lumps, but this is not essential at home.

Either serve immediately as an accompaniment to dishes such as roast cod, or reheat gently in a large saucepan over a low heat when needed.

Rosti Potatoes

Serves 6

*450 g (1 lb) roasting potatoes,
King Edward*

55 ml (2 fl oz) butter, melted

55 ml (2 fl oz) olive oil

salt and pepper

In Switzerland, the home of rosti, they cook the potatoes before grating them. I prefer to grate the potatoes raw. This is the recipe used in the Norfolk Asparagus with Rosti Potatoes, Streaky Bacon and Hollandaise (*see* recipe, page 71).

Method

Pre-heat the oven to 180C/350F/Gas 4.

Peel the potatoes and grate them coarsely. Place in a clean tea towel and wring out as much moisture as possible before placing them in a bowl. Add half the melted butter, season, and mix well. Heat a 20 cm (8 inch) non-stick frying pan, add the olive oil and the remainder of the melted butter. Put the grated potatoes into the frying pan and cook on a fairly high heat until the underside is browned. Remember to shake the pan so the potatoes do not stick. Next, turn the rosti over and continue to cook, shaking the pan occasionally, until the other side is browned.

Place the rosti in the pre-heated oven for 15–20 minutes, or until the potato is cooked right through. Remove from the oven and keep warm. Either serve immediately by slipping the rosti out of the pan and cutting into 6 or 8 wedges or leave the rosti in the pan and reheat it slowly when ready to serve. Try topping it with bacon and a fried egg before finishing with some grated Gruyere cheese for a hearty meal.

Rustic Ratatouille

Serves 8

2 red onions

1 large aubergine, the purple
Italian variety is best

2 yellow peppers

2 red peppers

3 courgettes

1 small fennel bulb

275 ml (½ pint) olive oil

1 clove of garlic, peeled and
roughly chopped

450 g (1 lb) baby vine tomatoes

25 g (1 oz) basil, roughly
chopped or torn

black pepper

coarsely ground sea salt

Served hot or cold, this all in one dish tastes as good as it looks. I prefer the vegetables cut into chunky pieces – that way you can taste all the individual ingredients.

Method

Pre-heat the oven to 220C/425F/Gas 7.

Peel the onions, cut into quarters and then cut each quarter lengthways again. Roughly chop the remaining vegetables, and put into a large bowl with the onions. Pour over the olive oil, add the garlic, and mix thoroughly with your hands. Spread out the vegetables in a roasting tin and season.

Place in the hot oven and, once the vegetables have started to colour, add the tomatoes and basil. Mix well and return to the oven for a further 20 minutes or so, until the vegetables are well coloured, but are still reasonably crunchy in texture. Check the seasoning and serve either hot or cold.

Sauteed Spinach with Spring Onions

Serves 4

50 g (2 oz) salted butter

1 bunch spring onions, roughly
chopped

350 g (12 oz) baby spinach,
washed

salt and pepper

Now that fresh, washed, baby spinach is widely available, this beautiful leaf vegetable has gained star status. A quick, simple dish.

Method

Heat the saucepan until very hot, and add the butter. It will foam immediately. At this point add the spring onions, followed by the spinach. Season. Treat the spinach as if you were stir-frying it and cook until it just starts to wilt. Remove from the heat and serve immediately.

Puddings

Puddings have to rank up there with my all-time favourite things: Norwich City Football Club and cricket. I have a *very* sweet tooth. Ask my dentist. I probably have more gold in my teeth than anywhere else I know, and that's not because I don't brush them – I really do just love puddings. And, it didn't help matters getting my first job in a professional kitchen in the pastry section. And that's where I ended up spending the next four years. Lucky old me...

One of the few times I have ever lost my rag in the kitchen was in fact over a pudding. A message came back from the dining room at Morston Hall that someone had claimed to have found mouldy bits in their creme brulee. The waitress produced the dessert plate as evidence: tiny brown specks had been scraped from the ramekin for me to see.

That was it. I stormed into the dining room, vanilla pod in hand, waving it in front of me for everyone to see, proclaiming loudly: 'This is a vanilla pod, and these are vanilla seeds, and your creme brulees were made this morning. Furthermore, anyone who knows me can vouch for the fact that I wouldn't normally behave this way.' Did I say that I'm *really* passionate about puddings?

Last but not least

The pastry section is probably the most artistic part of any kitchen: it is where you are allowed to let your creative skills take a flight of fancy. And, as the pudding course is the curtain call of any dining experience, we always want guests to leave on a memorable, dizzy high, wondering just how the pastry chef created such a work of art.

Despite all the intricate decorations and starry possibilities of a dessert plate, though, there's always room for the classics. You just can't beat a lemon tart, simply presented, no adornments, just unadulterated lemon tart. The same goes for vanilla pod creme brulee, a tarte tatin, or the smoothest, creamiest ice cream. Now you're talking.

Sorbets and ice creams

When I had a summer job on the beach in the south of France, I seem to recall spending more time sitting down and eating sorbets and ice creams than selling them. Before long, much to my dismay, my services were dispensed with. Nevertheless I'll always remember the flavour of the melon sorbet.

To this day I remain an ice cream and sorbet fanatic. Indeed, every night of the week at Morston Hall we serve a different one alongside the pudding. Consequently we need to buy a new machine at least twice a year – it's simply a case of the thing wearing out. However, you'll be relieved to hear that the recipes in this chapter can all be made successfully if you don't own an ice cream machine. All you need to do is freeze the mixture in a shallow container, but you must beat it thoroughly at least three or four times during the freezing process. Remember, the more you beat the ice cream mixture, the smaller the ice crystals become, and the smoother the end result.

Your other most important asset when making an ice cream or sorbet is your finger: you'll need it for tasting the mixture before it is frozen. For sorbets, you are aiming for a smack in the lips intensity of flavour, and there should be no doubt in your mind as to what the flavour of the fruit puree is exactly. The sorbet mixture also needs to be sufficiently sweet.

The rule for serving ice creams and sorbets is to take them out of the freezer at least 20 minutes before they are eaten. This allows them to come to a stage where scooping and serving is easier. And equally important is the fact that their flavour can be better appreciated if they are less solidly frozen.

Baked Alaska

Serves 8

For the sponge base

6 eggs, separated

160 g (5½ oz) caster sugar

175 g (6 oz) plain flour, sifted

For the Italian meringue

4 egg whites

225 g (8 oz) caster sugar

55 ml (2 fl oz) water

You will also need

1 litre (1¾ pint) tub of best

quality vanilla ice cream or,

better still, home-made

8 tbsp strawberry or raspberry

jam

25 x 30 cm (10 x 12 inch) tray

or a Swiss roll tin lined with

greaseproof paper

Method

Scoop 8 rounded balls of ice cream onto a plastic tray, that has been lined with clingfilm, and put into the freezer immediately.

To make the sponge, first pre-heat the oven to 200C/400F/Gas 6. Place the 6 egg whites in a spotlessly clean mixing bowl of a food mixer and whisk on a high speed until stiff. Gradually add the sugar. Once you have whisked it all in, add the egg yolks, one at a time.

Next, fold in the sieved flour with a slotted spoon. Spread the mixture evenly into the prepared Swiss roll tin, and bake in the hot oven for 10 minutes until springy to the touch.

Once the sponge has cooled, cut out 8 x 7.5 cm (3 inch) rounds with a pastry cutter. Next, hollow out a small circle with a spoon from the centre of each sponge round. Be extremely careful not to break right through the base by cutting too forcefully. Place the sponge rounds on a baking tray and fill the hollow with a spoonful of jam.

To make the meringue, place the egg whites in the clean bowl of a food mixer. Before turning on the mixer, bring the sugar and water to the boil over a medium heat in a thick-bottomed pan. Using a sugar thermometer, start to take the mixture to a temperature of 115C/240F. This will take about 5 minutes of boiling time. The moment the sugar reaches 110C/230F, turn on the mixer and start whisking the egg whites at high speed. Once the sugar reaches 115C/240F, pour it over the whisked egg whites very slowly and carefully while continuing to keep the mixer whisking. The meringue will have increased in size considerably. Leave the machine to continue whisking the mixture for approximately 5 minutes until it cools. This is a classic Italian meringue.

Finally, to cook the Baked Alaska, pre-heat the oven to 200C/400F/Gas 6. Remove the ice cream balls from the freezer, and place one on top of the jam in the centre of each of the sponge rounds. Cover the ice cream and sponge, from base to top, with the meringue mixture, making absolutely sure that the meringue coats all of the components. Using a fork, create a rough peaked finish with the meringue.

Place in the pre-heated oven for 4 to 5 minutes until the meringue is golden brown on top. Serve immediately with Creme Anglaise or pouring cream, and ideally a scattering of fresh Norfolk raspberries.

Classic Lemon Tart

Serves 6–8

250 g (9 oz) Sweet Pastry (see
*   recipe, page 32)*

2 egg yolks, beaten, for sealing
*   the pastry case*

7 eggs

275 g (10 oz) caster sugar

rind of two lemons, juice of four
*   lemons, kept separate*

225 ml (8 fl oz) double cream

25 cm (10 inch) fluted flan tin
*   with removable base.*

If I were allowed one pudding on my desert island, it would be this one. Enough said.

Method

Pre-heat the oven to 180C/350F/Gas 4.

Line a flan tin with pastry, cover with greaseproof paper and fill with baking beans or rice. Place in the pre-heated oven and bake blind until the pastry starts to brown around the edges. Remove from the oven, carefully lift out the greaseproof paper and the beans or rice, and return to the oven. Once the base starts to colour, remove from the oven and brush the pastry all over with the beaten egg yolks to seal any cracks. Return to the oven and bake until the yolk mixture is cooked. Repeat this process twice more to ensure that the pastry case is absolutely sealed. Remove from the oven and set aside.

Turn down the oven to 140C/275F/Gas 1.

To make the filling, gently whisk the eggs and sugar together in a bowl, without creating too many bubbles or froth. Add the lemon juice and the double cream, and pass the liquid through a sieve into a jug. Skim off any froth and finally stir in the lemon rind.

Place the warm pastry case onto a baking sheet and put it into the oven. Pour the lemon custard mixture into the pastry case there as it is hard to avoid spilling the mixture if you move it after it's been poured in. Cook for about 50 minutes until just set, although it should still wobble slightly in the middle. Remove from the oven and cool. Do not use the fridge as this will make your tart heavy in texture.

Creme Caramel with Sultanas

Traditionally made with just milk, I prefer enriching this recipe with half milk and half cream. The idea of adding the sultanas came about after lunching at Marco Pierre White's restaurant on Wandsworth Common many many years ago...

Method

Pre-heat the oven to 140C/275F/Gas 1.

Firstly make the caramel by dissolving the caster sugar in the water in a saucepan over a moderate heat. Bring to the boil. Watch carefully and once the boiling liquid turns a golden caramel colour, remove from the heat, and pour some into the bottom of each dariole mould. Next, add the soaked sultanas and set aside.

To make the cremes, lightly beat together the whole eggs, egg yolk and sugar in a large bowl. Split the vanilla pod in half lengthways with a sharp knife, and scrape the seeds into a saucepan. Add the cream, milk, vanilla extract and the vanilla pod. Bring the mixture just to boiling point over a moderate heat. Pour the hot milk over the eggs and sugar, and whisk thoroughly. Pass through a fine sieve into a pouring jug, and skim off any froth or bubbles.

Pour the custard into the dariole moulds and arrange in a roasting tin. Add boiling water to the roasting tin to halfway up the sides of the dariole moulds, and then cook in the pre-heated oven for about 50 minutes, until the cremes are just set. Remove from the roasting tin and allow to cool completely, preferably overnight.

To serve, loosen the cremes with a small knife, working your way around the sides. Turn out on to the centre of a serving plate, so that the caramel runs down the sides.

Serves 6

For the caramel

150 g (5 oz) caster sugar

55 ml (2 fl oz) water

50 g (2 oz) sultanas, soaked overnight in 25 ml (1 fl oz) rum

For the creme

4 eggs

1 egg yolk

150 g (5 oz) caster sugar

275 ml (½ pint) double cream

275 ml (½ pint) full-fat milk

1 tsp vanilla extract

1 vanilla pod

6 x 150 ml (¼ pint) dariole moulds, or ramekins

Egg Custard Tart

Serves 6–8

250 g (9 oz) Sweet Pastry (see

   recipe, page 32)

2 egg yolks, beaten, for sealing

   the pastry case

75 g (3 oz) caster sugar

8 egg yolks

570 ml (1 pt) double cream

freshly grated nutmeg

20 cm (8 inch) fluted flan tin

   with a removable base

This pudding is best made in the morning for eating in the evening as it really does not keep in the fridge. At Morston Hall we often serve a slice of this tart with fresh English raspberries or a scoop of Blood Orange Sorbet (see recipe, page 165).

Method

Pre-heat the oven to 180C/350F/Gas 4. Line the flan tin with the Sweet Pastry. Leave any excess pastry hanging over the edges: you will get a neater finish on the tart crust if you cut the pastry off after you have cooked the filling. Line the raw pastry case with greaseproof paper and fill with baking beans or rice to keep the pastry flat.

Place the pastry case in the pre-heated oven and bake blind until it starts to brown around the edges. Remove from the oven. Carefully lift out the greaseproof paper and baking beans before replacing the case in the oven.

Once the base starts to colour, remove from the oven and brush the pastry all over with the beaten egg yolks to seal any cracks. Return to the oven and, as soon as the egg yolk mix is cooked, repeat the process twice more to ensure that the pastry case is totally sealed. Finally, remove from the oven and set aside.

Turn the oven temperature down to 120C/250F/Gas ¾, and proceed by making the filling. Whisk the sugar and egg yolks together in a bowl. Bring the cream to the boil in a saucepan, then take off the heat and pour over the egg yolks and sugar, whisking well. Pass through a fine sieve into a jug, and skim off any bubbles from the surface.

To bake the tart, place the baked pastry case on a baking sheet and put it into the oven: it is much easier to fill the case in situ, as it is virtually impossible to move the filled base without spilling it. Carefully pour the filling into the case, grate nutmeg over the top, and bake for 45–50 minutes. Keep checking as the tart cooks. You are aiming for the filling to be just set, but still slightly wobbly in the centre.

At this point remove from the oven and leave to cool. Do not put in the fridge as this will alter the texture and make the tart heavy. Finally, just prior to serving, trim the pastry edges with a sharp knife.

Light and Dark Chocolate Torte

Serves 8–10

175 g (6 oz) digestive biscuits

25 g (1 oz) unsalted butter,
  melted

150 g (¼ pint) liquid glucose

juice and finely grated rind of
  1 orange

110 g (4 oz) caster sugar

225 g (8 oz) dark chocolate,
  64–70% cocoa solids

8 tbsp Cointreau

425 ml (¾ pint) double cream

225 g (8 oz) white chocolate

20 cm (8 inch) springform
  round cake tin

Method

Pre-heat the oven to 180C/350F/Gas 4.

Line the bottom and sides of the cake tin with greaseproof paper.

Crumble the biscuits in a food processor on a high speed before mixing them into the melted butter by hand. Press the biscuit mix into the lined baking tin, and bake for 10 minutes. Remove from the oven and leave to cool.

Mix the liquid glucose, orange juice and rind, and sugar in a saucepan and heat gently. Once the sugar has melted, bring to the boil and simmer for 2 minutes. Remove from the heat and set aside.

Break the dark chocolate into a bowl, add half the Cointreau, and melt together over a pan of barely simmering water. Next, stir half the warm orange and sugar mixture into the melted chocolate, and allow to cool.

Lightly whip the cream to the point where it should still leave a trail when the whisk is lifted. Next, gently fold half the whipped cream into the melted chocolate mixture and, once it is thoroughly incorporated, pour onto the biscuit base levelling it out with a palette knife. Allow to cool and then place in the fridge.

Repeat the process using the white chocolate, the remainder of the Cointreau and the whipped cream. When melting the white chocolate with the Cointreau do so very slowly as the texture will go grainy if it is mixed too quickly. Add the remaining orange and sugar mixture and then allow to cool. Next carefully fold in the remaining whipped cream. Pour the white chocolate mixture on top of the dark chocolate in the baking tin, smooth over the top and refrigerate.

To serve, unclip and remove tin, then place the chocolate torte onto a serving plate. To make slicing easy, use a knife that has been dipped into hot water and dried.

Panettone Creme Brulee

Serves 6

1 loaf of panettone

1 vanilla pod

425 ml (¾ pint) double cream

6 egg yolks

75 g (3 oz) caster sugar

6 tsp caster sugar to glaze

6 ramekins, 7.5 cm (3 inches)

Until one of the chefs in the kitchen suggested using panettone, the sweet Italian bread, I had never varied the way we prepared this all-time classic pudding. It is unusual in that it is turned out of the ramekin for serving.

Method

Pre-heat the oven to 140C/275F/Gas 1.

Cut 6 slices of panettone about 1 cm (½ inch) thick. Then, using a round pastry cutter the same size as the ramekins, cut 6 discs of panettone and place one in the bottom of each ramekin.

Using a sharp knife, cut the vanilla pod in half lengthways, and scrape the seeds into a saucepan. Then add the vanilla pod and double cream. Bring gently to the boil over a medium heat. Remove from the heat and set aside to infuse for 10 minutes.

Whisk the egg yolks and sugar in a bowl. Bring the cream nearly back to boiling and remove the vanilla pod. While still whisking the egg and sugar mixture, pour in the cream. Pass through a fine sieve into a jug, then pour a little of the strained liquid custard mixture into the ramekins, to cover the panettone. Leave for 5 minutes for the panettone to absorb the liquid, then top up. Don't worry if the panettone floats to the top at this stage, once the brulees are cooked and turned out, the panettone will be at the bottom.

Place the ramekins in a deep-sided roasting tin, and pour boiling water into the tin to about a third of the way up the ramekin dishes. Place in the pre-heated oven and cook for about 50 minutes until the brulees are firm, but still slightly wobbly in the centre when shaken. Remove from the oven, take the brulees out of the tin and allow to cool before chilling in the fridge.

To serve, dip the base of the ramekins in boiling water and go round them with a sharp knife, before giving them a good shake in cupped hands. Turn out the brulees onto a serving plate, bottom-side up. Scatter a teaspoon of caster sugar over the top of each brulee and glaze with a blowtorch until the tops turn a golden caramel colour.

Tarte Tatin

Serves 6–8

350 g (12 oz) puff pastry

6 Granny Smith apples

175 g (6 oz) unsalted butter

225 g (8 oz) caster sugar

23 cm (9 inch) diameter, deep-sided non-stick frying pan with a metal handle that can go into the oven

Classic French apple tart: puff pastry, caramelised sugar and apples, a dollop of double cream – there's little more to say. Remember though that Granny Smiths are the apples to use for this recipe as they do hold their shape once they are cooked.

Method

Pre-heat the oven to 220C/425F/Gas 7.

Roll out the puff pastry into a 30-cm (12-inch) diameter circle approximately 3 mm (⅛ inch) thick, making sure it is large enough to cover the frying pan. I use a large dinner plate as a guide. Lay the pastry on a tray, pricking it all over with a fork (*see* photo 1) and rest in the fridge until needed.

Peel, halve and core the apples (*see* photos 2 and 3). I find a melon baller is useful for coring them.

Pat the butter over the base of the frying pan and cover with the sugar. Working from the outside of the pan, pack the apples close together, pushing them, rounded-side down, into the sugar and butter (*see* photo 4). Over a moderate heat, allow the apples in the sugar and butter to caramelise to a light golden colour, watching carefully so that the apples do not burn (*see* photo 5).

Once you have an even caramel colour, remove the pan from the heat, and place the pastry over the apples (*see* photo 6). Gather together the overlapping edges of the pastry, tucking them down inside the pan. Place the frying pan in the pre-heated oven and cook for 20–25 minutes until the pastry is golden.

Remove from the oven and allow to rest for 5 minutes before turning the Tarte Tatin over on to a large serving plate. Serve with cream or homemade Vanilla Pod Ice Cream (*see* recipe, page 162).

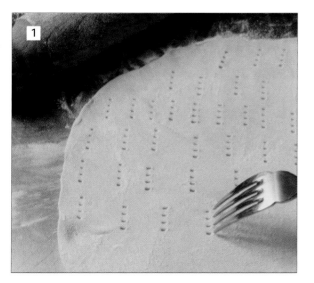

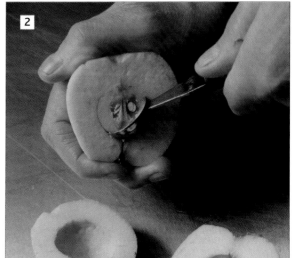

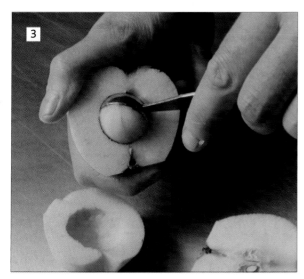

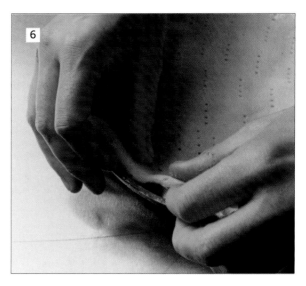

Vanilla Panna Cotta

This is an easy dessert that can be made a day in advance. Not good for the waistline though – but who cares. It is just as good alone or served with fresh, soft fruit such as raspberries, strawberries or apricots.

Serves 10

3 gelatine leaves

1 litre (1¾ pints) double cream

150 g (5 oz) caster sugar

2 vanilla pods

10 ramekins, 7.5 cm (3 inch)

Method

Put the gelatine leaves in a shallow dish with some cold water to soften. Heat the cream and sugar in a saucepan. With a sharp knife, split the vanilla pods lengthways and scrape out the seeds. Add these, together with the pods, to the cream. Bring to the boil, then remove from the heat.

Remove the gelatine leaves from the water, squeezing out any excess, and whisk into the hot cream and vanilla mixture so that it dissolves. Strain the mixture through a fine sieve into a large jug and allow to cool.

After about 45 minutes, and just before the custard sets, whisk the mixture again to disperse the vanilla seeds. Pour into the ramekins and leave in the fridge to set completely.

To serve, dip the base of the ramekins into boiling water, count to 5 and run a sharp knife around the edge to loosen before turning out the Vanilla Panna Cotta on to plates.

Pistachio Ice Cream

Serves 8

50 g (2 oz) unsalted, shelled
  pistachio nuts

1 vanilla pod

425 ml (¾ pint) double cream

6 egg yolks

150 g (5 oz) caster sugar

Method

Using a pestle and mortar, pound the pistachios to a paste. Alternatively, use a food processor.

Cut the vanilla pod in half lengthways with a sharp knife and scrape out the seeds. Add these with the vanilla pod to the cream and slowly bring to the boil in a saucepan. Once the liquid has boiled, remove from the heat, whisk in the pistachio paste and set aside to infuse.

Next, whisk the egg yolks and sugar in a large bowl, and add the warm, pistachio and vanilla-infused cream, whisking thoroughly. Remove the vanilla pod and return the mixture to the saucepan. Stir continuously over a moderate heat until the custard thickens sufficiently to coat the back of a spoon. Take care not to let it boil or the cream will curdle. Remove from the heat and pass through a sieve into a bowl.

Allow to cool, stirring occasionally, before churning in an ice cream machine. Serve immediately, or freeze in an airtight container.

Vanilla Pod Ice Cream

Serves 8

2 vanilla pods

570 ml (1 pint) double cream

275 ml (½ pint) milk

10 egg yolks

225 g (8 oz) caster sugar

Method

Cut the vanilla pods in half lengthways using a sharp knife and scrape the vanilla seeds into a saucepan. Add the cream, milk and the vanilla pods and, stirring frequently, bring slowly to the boil. Leave to infuse.

Meanwhile place the egg yolks and sugar in a large bowl, and whisk well with a hand-held electric whisk. While continuing to whisk the egg yolks and sugar, add the infused cream and milk (having removed the vanilla pods) to create a light custard. Pass the custard through a sieve, add back to the saucepan, and stir continuously over a low heat until the custard thickens sufficiently to coat the back of a spoon. Be cautious as you do this, as even heating the mixture a fraction too much will cause it to curdle. If, however, it does curdle, you can usually retrieve it by whizzing it up on the highest speed setting in a liquidiser. The consistency will be thinner, but useable.

Finally, pass the custard through a sieve, and allow to cool completely before churning to a soft consistency in an ice cream machine. Serve immediately, or freeze in an airtight container.

Blood Orange Sorbet (see photo opposite)

Serves 6

275 ml (½ pint) water

200 g (7 oz) caster sugar

425 ml (¾ pint) freshly
squeezed blood orange juice,
strained

juice of one lemon

Method

Gently bring the water and sugar to the boil in a saucepan, until all the sugar has dissolved. Simmer for about 5 minutes to make a stock syrup. Remove from the heat and add the orange and lemon juice. Stir well, strain through a sieve, and allow to cool completely before churning in an ice cream machine. Serve immediately, or freeze in an airtight container.

Granny Smith Sorbet

Serves 6

8 Granny Smith apples

juice of two lemons

110 g (4 oz) apricot jam

110 g (4 oz) caster sugar

55ml (2 fl oz) Calvados

Method

Without peeling and coring the apples, chop into 1 cm (½ inch) cubes and place in a blender, together with the lemon juice, apricot jam, caster sugar and Calvados. Blitz on a high speed before passing through a fine sieve to remove the pips and pulp. Churn immediately in an ice cream machine so the apples do not brown. Serve immediately, or freeze in an airtight container.

Pineapple Sorbet (see photo opposite)

Serves 8

1 large pineapple, peeled

225 g (8 oz) caster sugar

3 tbsp liquid glucose

425 ml (¾ pint) water

juice of one lemon

Method

Cut the pineapple into chunks. Put the sugar, liquid glucose and water into a saucepan and warm over a low heat until the sugar dissolves. Bring to the boil, and simmer gently for 5 minutes to make a stock syrup.

Add the pineapple chunks to the stock syrup, and gently poach over a low heat until soft. Pour into a liquidiser and whizz thoroughly before passing through a fine sieve into a bowl. Allow to cool, then add the lemon juice and stir well.

Once the mixture is cold, churn in an ice cream machine until it is firm. Serve immediately, or freeze in an airtight container.

Morston Hall Favourites

Buttered Norfolk Samphire

Serves 6

225 g (8 oz) freshly picked
  young samphire

pinch of sugar

40 g (1½ oz) unsalted butter

coarsely ground black pepper

a little good quality balsamic
  vinegar for serving

No cookery book from my backyard would be complete without featuring our local speciality – samphire – which is often incorrectly referred to as 'poor man's asparagus'. Believe me it is not: samphire is really rather delicious. In season from early July to mid August, this is when it makes its annual appearance on our menu. There are two ways of serving it: either pickled or eaten hot with butter and served with fish – the best way to eat the young, fresh samphire shoots as far as I'm concerned.

Method

Bring a large pan of water up to boiling point. Add a good pinch of sugar and plunge in the samphire. Boil for 2 minutes, before draining immediately. Refresh under cold running water.

Reheat in a saucepan over a medium heat with the butter and a good grinding of black pepper. To serve drizzle the balsamic vinegar over the samphire.

Herb Oil

75 g (3 oz) fresh mixed herbs,
  eg. coriander, parsley, basil
  and chervil, stalks removed

175 ml (6 fl oz) olive oil

1 clove garlic, peeled and
  crushed

salt and pepper

Add visual appeal and instant flavour to any number of salads, grilled meats or fish, by drizzling over a spoonful or two of herb oil. Use with discretion though as it is packed with flavour.

Method

Blanch the herbs in boiling, salted water for 2 minutes. Refresh immediately under cold running water, and squeeze dry in a clean tea towel. Mix the herbs in a blender together with the olive oil, garlic and seasoning to produce a vibrant green oil, pungent in flavour.

Seville Orange Marmalade

Makes 10 x 450 ml (1 lb) jars

1.35 kg (3 lb) Seville oranges

3 lemons

4 litres (7 pints) water

2.9 kg (6½ lb) preserving or

granulated sugar

a small knob of butter

10 x cleaned and sterilised jam

jars with tight fitting lids and

waxed discs

As with so many jam and marmalade recipes, this one has been handed down through my mother's family. The tradition continues to this day as every January we make about 500 jars in the Morston kitchen. Beware: a common fault is to over cook marmalade, which will quickly spoil its flavour. So when the 'wrinkle test' looks positive, take the marmalade off the boil immediately.

Method

Slice the oranges and lemons in half. Squeeze out as much juice as possible and strain into a jug, retaining the pips and any pith. Place the pips and pith into a piece of muslin and tie up tightly with string. Cut the orange and lemon skins into quarters and place these into a preserving pan together with the strained juice, the tied up pips and 4 litres (7 pints) of water.

Bring to the boil, and gently simmer until the liquid has reduced by half. This will probably take about 45 minutes. Once the liquid has been reduced, remove from the heat and allow to cool. When cool, remove the orange and lemon quarters and, with a sharp knife, slice very thinly.

Return the thinly sliced peel to the preserving pan, together with the sugar. Stir continuously over a low heat until the sugar has completely dissolved. Once the sugar has dissolved, turn up the heat and bring the mixture to the boil. When it reaches boiling point, keep the pan on a high heat, and retain a rolling boil for 15 minutes.

Finally, to test if the marmalade is at setting point, spoon a little of the hot marmalade onto a saucer and place in the fridge for a minute or so. If the surface of the cooled marmalade wrinkles when you run your finger through it, then the marmalade is ready. If not, carry on boiling and test every 5 minutes until it is ready.

When the marmalade is ready, remove from the heat and add a knob of butter to help reduce the formation of scum.

Either ladle or pour the marmalade into a jug so that it can easily be poured into the warmed jam jars. Seal immediately by placing a waxed disc on the top of the marmalade. Finally, once the marmalade is completely cool, seal the jam jars with a tight fitting lid.

Stewed Prunes

Serves 4

450 g (1 lb) Agen prunes,
* stones in*

1 orange, cut into quarters

1 cinnamon stick

110 g (4 oz) soft brown sugar

6 cloves

enough water to cover

Start the day the Morston way: stewed prunes really are delicious. I recommend ready-to-use Agen prunes for this recipe because they don't need soaking.

Method

Place all the ingredients into a large saucepan and cover with cold water. Slowly bring the pan to the boil, and simmer for about 20–25 minutes until the prunes are soft. Transfer to a large bowl. Cool, and store in the fridge.

Truffles

Dark, rich and always delicious, remember though truffles are only as good as the chocolate you use. Vary this recipe with white chocolate instead of dark, or Amaretto as a substitute for Grand Marnier.

Makes about 40 truffles

275 g (10 oz) dark chocolate,
* 70% cocoa solids*

275 ml (½ pint) double cream

40 g (1½ oz) unsalted butter

50 g (2 oz) caster sugar

4 tbsp Grand Marnier

extra chocolate for dipping

cocoa powder for dusting

petite four cases

Method

Break the dark chocolate into chunks and place in a large bowl. Combine the cream, butter, sugar and Grand Marnier in a saucepan and gently bring to simmering point, stirring occasionally. Then immediately pour it over the chocolate in the bowl, stirring continuously to a smooth consistency. Allow to cool before placing in the fridge overnight to set firmly.

Next, use a melon baller to scoop out little truffle balls from the set mixture, and arrange carefully on a sheet of greaseproof paper.

Holding the truffles on the end of a fork, dip them into a little melted chocolate before setting back onto the greaseproof paper to harden. Alternatively, dust them with cocoa powder. Finally, place in petite four cases ready for serving.

Morston Hall Vinaigrette

5 tbsp red wine vinegar

1 tbsp Dijon mustard

1 tbsp honey

1 tsp soft brown sugar

1 large clove of garlic, crushed

1 tsp salt

a good grinding of pepper

275 ml (½ pint) quality olive oil

150 ml (¼ pint) sunflower oil

herbs of your choice, finely

  chopped

Every time I make a salad dressing I am reminded of the wise words of my early mentor, the inimitable John Tovey: 'Your finger is the most important utensil you've got'. He was referring to the fact that a really good vinaigrette requires careful tasting as it is made. Once prepared, though, it will keep in an airtight jar in the fridge for up to a week. I suggest making up the basic mixture and adding fresh herbs as you go, to give salads a different twist.

Method

Whizz together the vinegar, mustard, honey, sugar, garlic, salt and pepper in a liquidiser or in a bowl using an electric hand held whisk. Mix the olive oil and sunflower oil in a jug and with the machine still running slowly pour in. Continue for a few more seconds, stop the machine and taste.

Depending on how you would like the vinaigrette to taste, now is the time to make adjustments. Don't be afraid to experiment. If it is too sharp, add a little more sugar or honey; perhaps it requires more seasoning; maybe it needs to be more zingy, so add some lemon juice or maybe a little fresh ginger.

Finally, and as near to serving as possible, add the fresh herbs, such as parsley, basil, marjoram or chives.

Basil vinaigrette works well over tomatoes; chive vinaigrette tastes good with new potatoes; and marjoram vinaigrette partners young salad leaves.

Onion Marmalade

Serves 4

2 tbsp olive oil

2 large onions, peeled and very

  thinly sliced

2 tbsp brown sugar

2 tbsp red wine vinegar

salt and pepper

Sweet, yet savoury this makes a great accompaniment to roast beef or Pan-fried Calves Liver (see recipe, page 119). In the Morston kitchen we often add a heaped tablespoon of onion marmalade to our White Bread Rolls (see recipe, page 27), in order to create a sweet onion bread.

Method

In a large saucepan heat the oil, add the sliced onions and cook over a high heat until well browned. Add the sugar and vinegar. Turn the heat down and continue cooking until the liquid has evaporated and the onion marmalade has become a rich, dark brown colour. Season to taste and serve.

Parsley Pancakes

Makes 12 pancakes

110 g (4 oz) plain flour

½ tsp sugar

1 egg

350 ml (12 fl oz) full-fat milk

1 tbsp butter, melted

3 tbsp parsley, chopped

salt and pepper

vegetable oil for cooking the

* pancakes*

These are an essential part of Loin of Venison en Croute (*see* recipe, page 115) because they soak up the juices of the meat and allow the pastry to stay crisp. Having made too many pancakes on one particular occasion, we discovered they worked as a savoury crepe to wrap around tips of blanched asparagus which we then smothered with hollandaise sauce. Waste not want not.

Method

Sift the flour, sugar and seasoning into a bowl. Make a well in the centre, and drop in the egg and half the milk. Whisk well to incorporate the flour. Next, add the rest of the milk and continue to whisk thoroughly. Sieve the mixture into a jug, and chill in the fridge for half an hour.

Immediately before you are ready to make the pancakes, stir the melted butter and chopped parsley into the batter.

Heat a teaspoon of vegetable oil in a 20 cm (8 inch) non-stick frying pan, swirling the oil around the pan. Pour off any excess. Using 2 fl oz of the pancake batter at a time, pour it into the frying pan and immediately swirl around the pan to create a thin pancake. Cook for about 30 seconds before flipping the pancake over and cooking for a further 30 seconds on the other side. Slide the cooked pancake onto a plate and continue to repeat the process until you have used all the batter. Serve the pancakes immediately. Alternatively, if you wish to prepare ahead, interleave the cooked pancakes with greaseproof paper and freeze.

Porridge

Serves 4

75 g (3 oz) porridge oats

570 ml (1 pint) full-fat milk

10 g (½ oz) unsalted butter

a pinch of salt

a little cream

For the most wonderful creamy porridge, soak the oats overnight and use all milk. Even in summer, it amazes me how many guests order porridge. Say no more.

Method

Begin the night before by mixing the oats in a bowl with the milk and a pinch of salt. Leave overnight in the fridge.

Cook the porridge the following morning on a very low heat, until the oats are soft and taste cooked. You may need to add a little more milk if the porridge is too thick. Just before serving, stir in the butter and pour over a little cream and, for real indulgence, a tot of malt whisky.

Index

Page numbers in *italics* refer to the illustrations